COLD TURKEY

LEFTOVERS

John W Ingalls MD

Enjoy Cold Turkey -

John Ingalls -

Acknowledgements

I will take responsibility for the mess contained within these covers but there are many who have inspired me to create it. I am thankful to God who makes all things possible. My life, like this collection essays is aimless enough. I am grateful for a shepherd to prod me out of the briars and back onto the path.

Secondly I am eternally grateful for my loving and forgiving wife, Tammy. If I am the book, she is the bookends, holding it all together. I have frequently made decisions based on the premise that it is easier to ask forgiveness than it is to ask permission. With her I have asked for much forgiveness and she has been kind enough to bestow it upon me, more than I have deserved.

From each of my children I have received far more than I have ever given. Over the years I have attempted to dole out parental wit and wisdom and now I am delighted to know they have all turned out to be wonderful people in spite of my efforts. Their grace, wisdom and character never fail to astound me. Perhaps my contribution has been, at times, an example of what not to become. Again their wonderful mother is the set of bookends to hold us together. Leah, Anna, Abigail and Billie Kay have each contributed to these pages in ways that most will never fully appreciate. Their personalities and lives have delighted and challenged me for the past 30 some years and they helped shape me as much as I have shaped them. I have decided to be nice to them because some day they may pick out my nursing home.

Each of my grandchildren has been a never ending source of delight. Ella B, Lilyanne, Eva Judy, Gracie and Caleb never fail to bring a smile to my face and delight to my heart. I am also secretly amused when their antics bring a bit of frustration to their parents, the same way we were frustrated in years past. The nut doesn't fall far from the tree.

Numerous teacher, mentors and friends, too many to mention at the risk of missing and offending, I will limit this to just one person. Dr. Richard Swenson MD has been a part of my life more than he will ever know. As a physician mentor he challenged and shaped the way in which I now administer medical counsel. However, his mentorship as an individual has meant much more. He has taught me to keep some margin in my life and that has made a world of difference.

I am thankful for the hundreds and perhaps thousands of people who have touched my life in simple ways. The impact of close friendships and casual acquaintances can never be underestimated. As a physician I have the awesome privilege of having an open window view into the lives of many. I have learned as much from them as I hope they have learned from me. I was once asked what kind of work I do. I explained that I don't actually work; I just sit around and talk with friends all day.

Finally I am very grateful to Gary King and Carl Heidel and the entire staff of the Inter-County Leader newspaper. They correct my mistakes and provide an avenue in which I was able to tell these stories and hopefully brighten someone's day just a bit. They have graciously allowed me to reprint these stories which first appeared in the Inter-County Leader.

Introduction

I never started out to write a book, at least not this book. It isn't really a book, more like a mulligan stew of experiences, ideas and phrases. Anyway it started from humble beginnings, with a pot of beans. It was a cold January day and I had nothing of importance to accomplish and that was the problem. For those of you who think they know me, idle time is dangerous time, sort of like playing with matches. I hatched the idea of cooking a pot of homemade baked beans in a cast iron dutch oven, in our wood burning fireplace. I won't ruin the story, you can read it later. Anyway it didn't actually work out as planned.

"Beans at 20 Below" was the beginning of the book but no one really knew it at the time; we were too busy cleaning up the mess. Inspired by my lack of prowess as a fireplace chef, I simply recorded the story and sent it off to a friend, proudly recalling my afternoon's misguided adventure. Unknown to me, he had forwarded my story on to the editor of the "Inter-County Leader" a small rural weekly paper covering several counties in northern Wisconsin.

The next week I was stunned to find my article complete with a photo on the front page of the paper. Certainly there could not have been anything noteworthy in the world that week I figured they were desperate for copy to fill the void. The presidential inauguration made page two.

Sometime later that year, I was invited to participate in a weekly column entitled "Community Voices" in which readers were asked to contribute topics of interest to the weekly paper with a community focus. I was enthusiastic about the idea and began submitted more ideas and stories than was required. The editor began running more and more of my stories until the general focus and intent of the column became diluted. It was no longer "Community Voices" but had become my own sounding board, something I never intended.

That projected ended and my writing was limited to recording my own personal mishaps and adventures. I wrote purely for enjoyment and never had any thought that I could or should write for commercial reasons. Many readers commented on how they enjoyed my essays, especially on how they could relate to them on a personal level. It was sometime later that Gary King (editor of Inter-County Leader), contacted me about starting my own column. Many had asked for more stories but I had to come up with a title for the column. For me that was the hardest part.

I contemplated many titles but nothing really suited the focus of the column. Actually the column had no focus. As a physician I felt an obligation to provide something of benefit to my readers or at the very least, not lead anyone astray. Yet the focus was not medicine or health related matters even though it was included in many of my stories.

One day, while discussing options to assist someone in quitting their smoking addiction, we mentioned the phrase "cold turkey". An obvious question jumped into my brain, "Where did the phrase originate and why"? "Cold Turkey" had various meanings and was a noun, a metaphor and an idiom rolled up together. In short, it was the perfect name for my column because it is what it is and nothing more.

As the column evolved, I came to realize that my words were in a sense a compliment to my efforts as a physician. In my office I tried to dispense wisdom along with appropriate medications and procedures and like most physicians I was right most of the time. Many people have let me know how they looked forward to receiving the paper each week and reading "Cold Turkey" was the first place they turned. In a simple way it provided an uplifting experience and a brief respite from the routine chores of daily living. I was reminded of a Bible verse, "A cheerful heart is good medicine, but a crushed spirit dries up the bones." Proverbs 17:22.

I have been asked why I write these stories and I can't actually say a clear and concise reason. Fish swim, birds fly, geese honk, painters paint, bakers bake and writers write. I guess I do it because I can't really find a reason not to. I fear that I have created a monster of sorts. What started as a simple distraction has grown to proportions beyond my control. Many have encouraged me to continue writing indefinitely because of their enjoyment or respite from the chores of live.

I believe there is value in the story itself beyond any lesson or parable. That is why children and grandchildren snuggle up beside you on the couch or in the big easy chair and ask for bedtime stories. That is why we get lost in the pages of a good novel, laughing, crying or becoming angry with the characters now indelibly embossed into our own lives. Stories of all kinds help us to live beyond the limited confines of our own existence. Stories help us to understand or experience events from another's perspective. Stories beg to be told.

I have a family heritage in writing. Laura Ingalls Wilder certainly left her mark on the world by telling simple stories about her family's pioneer existence. What they did was no different than thousands of other families and individuals during the formative years of this country. What she did differently was write those stories down for the enjoyment of her family and other readers. The value was in the story itself.

My daughter, Abigail has also beaten me to the press. She is a delightful author and has also published a children's book "Ella B and the Snippety Snappety Scissors" available through lulu.com. I think she would also agree that writers write because they really can't do otherwise.

If what I have written benefits one or two then my goal is already accomplished. Most people enjoy them because they see a small portion of themselves in the pages. These stories may be unique in the details but most of the circumstances are something to which we can all relate. What parents haven't been tired and frustrated at mealtime with complaining children? What person alive hasn't complained about the weather? Who hasn't had some nagging or concerning health issue that required more than a home remedy? What husband or wife hasn't been frustrated trying to understand the motives or actions of their spouse? What father hasn't worried about the questionable boy intent on dating his daughter?

Where will it go from here? I'm not sure. I don't labor under any illusions of grandeur. If it cheers you heart then rejoice. If it makes you think, then think. If it helps you start fires or you use it to wrap dead fish, then at least it has served a useful purpose. Read it, enjoy it and pass it on but keep a copy in the bathroom. You can get some serious reading done there and no one will bother you.

Cold Turkey, the Beginning

After two years as a successful columnist in a weekly newspaper, Inter-County Leader, I entered the digital age of publishing my own blog, dispensing my prescriptions for a better life. In this manner I was originally asked to give my column a new name; a name embracing the depths of wisdom and shameless wit that I employ. I have chosen a name with a multiplicity of meanings and variety of flavors, a name that may mean different things to different people depending on the context, a name we can all relate to in some fashion, "Cold Turkey".

Cold Turkey is what's left over after a holiday feast. The centerpiece of the meal revisited without all the fluff. In order to really enjoy cold turkey you have to be creative. You may have to invent dishes to get the full benefit of leftover cold turkey. To many it is the best part of the holiday feast, the time to enjoy the food at your own leisure when the relatives have returned home. It is just as satisfying and nutritious as the original meal without the social overtones. It's a metaphor representing the enjoyment of simple pleasures.

Cold Turkey is also an idiom. When we quit "cold turkey" we do it with decisiveness and conviction. There is no easing into a situation when we go "cold turkey" no sir; it's head first all the way. It embodies a general sense of determination to see any given situation through to its completion. "Cold Turkey" is "off the wall". If you tried to translate this into a different language it would end in total confusion. As you read that last statement you understood what I meant but in order to translate it successfully you would have to explain that words have many possible meaning and words organized into phrases may have layers of meanings and seldom are they literal.

Cold Turkey is or hopefully will be somewhat of a paradox. If the responses to my previous essays are any indication, then this blog should garner similar interest. While I wouldn't say the essays were "hot" there have been a substantial number of people that have called, wrote or stopped me on the street to offer their support. I believe that many will enjoy the content because it is something most of us can relate to on a personal level. While I attempt to dispense some information that has value, I frequently use myself as an example. I eat too much, I don't exercise as I should, I spill my coffee, I forget names of people and I say thing that I shouldn't say at the wrong times. I want you to see that sometimes the best advice doesn't come from someone who has it all together but often it comes from someone who can share the frustrations of daily existence and know how hard life can be at times.

Cold Turkey is a food and those of you who know me, know that I like food and like to talk about food. It will be "Killer Beets" and "Beans at 20 Below" stirred together with social commentary and medical advice. I don't believe in fast food, so chew it slow and share it with friends.

Cold Turkey is a paradox, an idiom and a metaphor served up in bite sized chunks. You can enjoy it in your bathrobe and slippers, chewing thoughtfully on the content or just spit it out if it doesn't agree with you.

Reading Cold Turkey is a bit like driving down a one way street, the wrong way. It may not always be right but it may give you different view than what you have experienced in the past. Most people quit "cold turkey" but this is where I start.

Beans at 20 below

Sometimes the joy of a season wears a bit thin. August heat and humidity often produces a longing for the first cool day of autumn, that first day you can wear a flannel shirt comfortably. Winter is like that as well. About the 3rd week of January I begin to lose the joy of winter and start thinking seriously about spring. Thankfully, in the mail, we begin to receive spring fishing, gardening and camping catalogs before the last Christmas ornament is stored away.

Today was a good example. A bright and cold Saturday in January, I brewed a pot of strong coffee and pondered my existence. Nearly 20 below zero the thermometer read. Thoroughly content after my third cup of black coffee, 3 slices of French toast dripping with butter and blueberry syrup and apple jam and a few well browned sausages, I began to think about camping in the summer. Campfires are always a big part of camping so I built a good fire in the open fireplace and settled into my chair with a spring Cabela's catalog.

I browsed through the fishing section, not finding anything that I didn't already have I proceeded into the camping section. Camp cooking is something we all aspire to and some even succeed. I am great with a Canadian shore lunch. Browned walleye fillets, sizzling potatoes with onions and a can of steaming hot beans round out the usual menu. Add in a cold drink or two and you have a meal fit for any king or queen.

The camp cooking photos in the catalog displayed gourmet meals without soot or smudge, deceptive to be sure, but inviting none the less. I checked the outdoor thermometer and it now hovered nearer to 10 below zero. The crackling fire in the fireplace beckoned.

Why not, I thought. I could try some campfire cooking in the house with my new dutch oven. I have cooked a lot of things over a fire. Once when I was trapping, a number of years ago, I even cooked and ate a blue jay. I don't recommend it. Today I decided to try my hand at baked beans. Not the kind from a can, no I wanted to make the variety my

Grandma used to make in a crock, in a wood fired cook stove. The kind that smelled of molasses, brown sugar and smoked bacon. The kind that dripped brown sweet juice down your chin. The kind of beans that produced sweet reminders of your meal for at least two days. That's the kind I was going to make over the fire.

I dug out my wife's recipe that had been given to her by a member of the older generation; someone who could appreciate honest slow cooking and real homemade food. Two pounds of navy beans, nearly a pound of cut up smoked bacon, water, onion, seasonings, brown sugar, dripping black strap molasses and a dash of dried mustard. Stirred together in the big cast iron dutch oven, I grinned. There would be music tonight!

The fire was bit hot so I donned some gloves and raked the coals around until I had a glowing bed of embers on which to place the dutch oven. I shoveled some coals onto the lipped lid of the pot and then carefully laid additional split firewood on the edge of the fire. This was an all day affair so I had to keep the fire going. A good pot of beans often took 6-7 hours of cooking time.

I was thoroughly satisfied. Slipping into my sheepskin moccasins, I brewed a pot tea and then searched my bookshelf for a new book. Occasionally poking at the fire, I added wood as needed. Pausing between chapters I decided it was time to check the beans and add a little water so they wouldn't dry out. As I swept some of the ash and coals off of the lid, I could smell the beans cooking. My wife was going to be so proud of me. She was a bit skeptical of the whole process but I knew I would gain her confidence after the peek under the lid.

I lifted the incredibly heavy cast iron pot out of the fireplace and onto the hearth. Using one of the fireplace tools I carefully lifted off the lid so to avoid any ashes contaminating the pot of beans. My visions of bubbling brown sauce juice covering the deep pot of beans and chunks of smoky bacon were dashed. No they weren't dashed, they were utterly destroyed. Armageddon wouldn't look this bad. Half of the beans were hard black pellets, much you would find along a rabbit trail after a forest fire. The other half of the beans were welded together into a vast round black brick with the burnt sugar and molasses being the cement that held it all together. My wife smiled and said nothing.

The rock hard concoction would have to be chiseled out of the pot. At 10 below zero outside I didn't look forward to the task. Perhaps a soaking would help. I dumped a big pot of water into the still very hot dutch oven. Big mistake! The petrified blackened beans became rapidly energized with the sudden production of steam. Not only was my supper ruined but I was now facing a burnt bean volcano! Mount St Helens was nothing compared to this. Well, that was a bit of an exaggeration but at least Mt St Helens didn't erupt in my living room.

I grabbed the steaming scorching cast iron pot and ran for the door. Ashes and reconstituted burnt bean juice marked my trail. A scoop of snow and 10 below weather helped quiet the eruption. I was humbled. Hiking through knee deep snow I deposited the burnt bean bricks behind the shed where the dog wouldn't likely find it and I returned to the house. My wife, God bless her, asked if I had learned a lesson. I nodded quietly as I swept the ashes and mopped up the remains of the volcano.

Scraping and scrubbing, I finally got the dutch oven cleaned out. Now mid afternoon, it was too late to try another pot of beans, not that anyone would let me try anyway however, I was able to salvage some personal pride. I convinced the family to let me try something else in the fireplace. A joint effort this time, we peeled apples and mixed up a batch of apple cobbler. Carefully tending the fire, ninety minutes later we were rewarded with crusty brown pastry coated apple cobbler, oozing with sweet sticky juice, topped with a scoop of vanilla ice cream. I was redeemed.

My wife was happy, the kids were happy and I was happy. There is nothing like beans at 20 below to really bring a family together.

Feeding Children

One of the most frustrating jobs of being a parent is mealtime. You can plan, shop, prepare and serve nutritious and delicious meals and 9 out of 10 times they will prefer the dog food. As kids grow up they put some of the most obnoxious things in their mouths repeatedly but put a dish of peas or tuna noodle casserole within three feet of them and they go into uncontrolled gagging. Apparently the sand coated bubblegum that they shared with the dog was more appetizing.

It is especially frustrating after a busy or challenging day at work. After a long day at work you went to the grocery store, wandered the isles looking for something quick, easy, nutritious and acceptable to an age range of 4 to 40 years. Deep in your mind you knew that it didn't matter what you chose. A frozen pizza or a box of mac and cheese was always a safe backup. After jockeying the grocery cart up and down the aisles with other equally tired and frustrated parents you somewhat reluctantly wandered toward home. A skilled parent would somehow entertain starving children while deftly turning away their efforts to snack on junk food as the meal was being prepared. While ignoring barking dogs, complaining children, smoke alarms and phone calls the mother (usually the mother but not always) serves a well prepared delicious and nutritious meal in near record time.

The meal conversations usually begin with "What's that smell?" "I'm not hungry" "Does this have onions in it?" "I am going over to Bobby's for pizza and a movie later." "Why can't I have pizza too?" and so on. You plead, argue, bribe and threaten your children to just try a taste of what is before them but to no avail. Already weakened from a busy day and beaten lower by the cutting remarks from the surly mob at the table, you give in and serve Oreo cookies and milk. The dream of just one peaceful meal is quickly reconciled with reality. The food prepared is now resigned to the leftover bin in the refrigerator until it sprouts and then it will be delivered to the compost pile.

Over the years my wife and I have gotten much smarter. Rather than wasting time shopping, preparing, cooking, serving and arguing and then throwing it away we now do it more efficiently. After shopping we just throw it away.

Working in health care and dispensing advice on feeding children is a tricky thing for me. Nowhere is the adage more true, "Do as I say and not as I do." When my oldest was born, we were firmly into the organic foods all natural lifestyle. She never ate sugar until she was a toddler. Attired in soft soled moccasins she would pull home grown carrots from the garden, wipe the dirt on her pants and eat them all the way to the stem. Later, after refusing her mother's home made lentil soup she would emulate the chipmunks and stuff her cheeks with dog food and maybe even drink out of the dog's water dish.

Twelve years later with good intentions but different tactics we have introduced our last child into the world of fine dining. She knows that McDonalds, KFC, Pizza Hut and Dunkin' Donuts are the four food groups. If we return home from work late, no worries. Our youngest children have already eaten a bag of chips and salsa and a pan of brownies.

I won't ever pretend to have all the answers, in fact I have quite a few questions myself. With my children all now leading vibrant healthy lives and making healthy food and lifestyle choices I am actually amazed. They have turned out remarkably well despite my own lack of understanding or leading by example.

This may seem like I don't care, but I really am an advocate for nutrition and good food. Both my wife and I do our best to model acceptable behavior and healthy choices, not only in dining but in life as well. Our food choices lean more toward slow food than fast food. We encourage our children to make their own choices and prepare meals for themselves and others. We expose them to a wide variety of foods available not only from here but those with origins in other countries and cultures as well (Try squid fried rice for breakfast in Thailand or grilled chicken feet!) We also try to respect their dislikes and don't force the issue, (some people just hate liver).

I think I have learned the most through the parenting process. In fact when you finally think you have it figured out you realize you are now a grandparent. Maybe that is why Grandma gives you cookies before meals, helps you make mud pies and lets you share your ice cream cone with the dog. My best advice to young parents, relax; your children with likely turn out just fine in spite of your best efforts.

Becoming Grandparents

This article was originally written a couple of years ago but it deserves to be dusted off and reprinted. I can say without reservation that the honorable titles of Grandma and Grandpa or any variation of which you choose cannot be outdone. We have been blessed with the presence of Ella, Lily, Eva, Caleb and Grace. They have enriched our lives in ways that are impossible to imagine.

Nothing prepared me for the role of being a grandfather. Mentally and emotionally I wasn't ready to accept the role. Physically I wasn't old enough, after all aren't grandpas and grandmas old and gray and slightly bent at the knees and back? I still had years before I could realistically consider retirement, I had a daughter in high school and I still had the mind of an 18 year old. Then I looked in the mirror. What looked back at me was a shock. I now looked like every grandfather should look. I had gray hair for that distinguished look, a lightly expanded abdomen for that successful look and hemorrhoids for that concerned look. Maybe I was ready to be a grandpa. On the other hand my loving wife was ready for the role of grandmother but she didn't look the part. Appearing 20 years younger than myself and sometimes mistaken for being my daughter she was ready to embrace her grandchildren with open arms.

Grandmothers are like mothers with a little seasoning. They have the unique ability to blend together love, forgiveness and a bit of discipline into a big bowl with some sugar and it always comes out looking like warm chocolate chip cookies and cold milk. Grandmothers and food almost always go hand in hand. Maybe that is why we eat when we experience stress because it subconsciously reminds us of the unconditional love that our grandmothers bestowed upon us. Even today the smell of some foods will trigger memories of my grandmothers cooking up huge pots of baked beans, pancakes or big turkeys for Thanksgiving or Christmas.

While grandmothers may be identified with a certain degree of reverence, grandfathers are often associated with character. Grandfathers sometimes have nick names such as "Gramps" or "Papa" but just as likely they may be known as "Crazy old Coot", "Geezer" or "Old Goat". These nick names often reflecting their own level of character development. Grandfathers also have two other traits that set them apart from grandmothers, the ability to tell stories over and over and over again and the second is the ability to stretch the honest truth beyond the breaking point.

Visits to Grandpa's and Grandma's house often follow a similar pattern. I see similarities from my childhood replayed in my children's experiences and now with my own grandchildren as they visit us. Grandma would meet you at the door with hugs and adoring comments about your new shoes or how your hair cut looked, quickly followed by comments such as, "My you kids look hungry, want something to eat?" It didn't matter what your parents said because Grandma was going to feed you anyway. You didn't dare to not eat because that might offend Grandma and maybe the next time she wouldn't make your favorite cake or cookies.

Grandma was almost always the first to greet you at the door, but Grandpa was more reserved or lazy. He would be waiting in his easy chair and would call out to you "Come here you little whipper-snapper", he would mess up your new haircut with his big hands and then pause. "Say, did I ever tell you about the time...?" You always knew what was coming because Grandpas can't remember if they told the story before and each time it was told the truth got stretched enough that it was never quite the same story anyway. When you are in preschool or grade school ages you listened politely and even beg for more stories. When you got a bit older you learned how to discreetly roll your eyes when listening to these stories. My Dad is a classic story teller and he has told enough tall tales that I noticed it was starting to affect my children. They rolled their eyes back so much that I thought they were coming loose. One of my kids can now move her eyes independent of each other like an iguana. I guess she can thank her Grandpa for that.

When I first became a grandpa it frightened me. I wasn't old enough or wise enough to be a grandfather. I couldn't stretch the truth and repeat myself like a real grandpa could. And then one day it happened. My granddaughter Ella climbed up onto my lap, she gave me part of her cookie from grandma and said, "Grandpa, will you tell me a story?"

I cleared my throat, thought for a moment and then as natural as ever I began, "Did I ever tell you about the time…" I glanced down at her in time to see her smile at Grandma and then roll her eyes ever so slightly.

Heavenly Bratwurst

As a mental exercise, one evening at dinner, we discussed what meal you would select if you knew it was your last meal. It may seem a bit morbid but actually the focus was on the food part and not on the dying part. Having the knowledge in which this would be your last meal made most of us in attendance lean toward elite, expensive or exotic dishes. Filet mignon led the list with grilled lobster making an appearance as well. I voted for grilled bratwurst and beans.

Maybe it is the German heritage I possess or perhaps it is my football tailgating memories that force my decisions but bratwurst properly prepared ranks as a delicacy. A sputtering, flaming bratwurst on the grill lifts the spirits. Nothing announces the arrival of summer quite the same way. Lifting the cover up from the grill you are accosted with smoke and a flare of flames licking at the meat. It gets in your eyes as the heat warms you face and you can't help but smile and feel incredibly fortunate at your circumstances. Bratwurst goes straight to the heart.

Actually medical research has tried to frighten us away from grilled meat, processed meat in particular. Recently there was a study released that seemed to indicate that one out of nine deaths could be directly related to red meat consumption with processed meat leading the charge. One out of ten deaths attributed to red meat is frightening but when viewed from another perspective it is almost apocalyptic. That means nine out of ten people die from eating fruits and vegetables! While eating your bratwurst, make sure you go easy on the sauerkraut.

While I try to eat reasonably healthy, I am not always the best example. I tend to enjoy chocolate chip cookies and milk as well. If my wife allows me one after dinner, I will take two when she isn't watching and another before bedtime. If she finds out, I try to explain how the fruits and vegetables are the real killers. In my defense I try to explain, how in the studies which were done with red meat, the researchers failed to take into account how much ketchup and mustard was used. That may be the real problem. What if we find out that 10 out of 10 people die from eating fruits and vegetables?

I have at times had issues with other dietary issues as well. On a couple of occasions I have put my foot in my mouth, figuratively of course, but it still doesn't help the diet. Usually I have to follow it up with a few chocolate chip cookies to help me feel better. With one individual I made a serious error in judgment, not in my diagnosis and treatment plan, but in my response to her questions. She presented with a skin condition, about which, I wasn't familiar. I asked the usual questions about the problem including what, where, when, why and how. I also inquired about what she had already tried. I struck out on every point and was unable to identify her problem or offer a definitive solution.

"What do you think it is?" was her logical response. I puzzled for a moment and unable to contrive an education response I simply gave an honest reply. "I don't know, but we'll find out at the autopsy." As soon as I spoke, I regretted my words but it was too late. My foot was firmly planted in my mouth and I struggled to mumble an apology. She was shocked, then laughed and then forgave me.

Actually the medical studies should be repeated to determine how many people die from eating crow, or sticking their foot in their mouth, or even eating humble pie. It might be as dangerous as eating fruits and vegetables. I certainly wouldn't pick crow or humble pie as my final dining experience.

I am sticking with bratwurst and beans as my final meal. Watching them sizzle on the grill, it makes me happy. With each bite of the hot, juicy, greasy sausage covered up with sauerkraut, spicy brown mustard and some ketchup I am just one step closer to heaven.

Going to the Dogs

Since the beginning of civilization dogs have been regarded as man's best friend. They have become embedded in the social fabric of our families to the point that we bestow upon them human characteristics. They are included in family photos and vacation plans and when they die we erect markers or stones to identify their graves. Some pet owners have gone as far as taking their dear departed pet to the taxidermist so Rover or Rex will always be there to greet them at the door or be eternally at rest by the master's chair.

Primarily dogs but also cats or other pets, have been used metaphorically to describe our experiences. If someone experiences a flu bug we call into work sick, but if we are really suffering we let everyone know we are sicker than a dog. Then we lie about the house feeling dog tired and read our favorite dog eared book. We watch our favorite sports teams on television and when they struggle we complain that they are no dog-gone good and they are going to the dogs. We can fight like cats and dogs, we can't do our work outside if it is raining cats and dogs and if you have a wild idea about going to the cat house you will actually end up in the dog house in the end.

We all know it's a dog eat dog world out there and if you want to run with the big dogs, especially if you want to be top dog you are going to have to work like a dog to get there. Even if you are an old sea dog you have value and can contribute to society, but if you want to excel in your chosen pursuit in life you need to start young because everyone knows you can't teach an old dog new tricks.

There are hunting dogs, lap dogs, work dogs, show dogs and dogs that defy categories. Pure bred dogs identified by papers outlining their pedigree can command high prices but those with a diverse genetic background are generally regarded as mutts. No matter what breed or mix of dog you might have you will discover an almost universal characteristic among your canine family members, unconditional acceptance.

Reggie White is our dog and he is nothing like the famous Packer football player he was named after. In dog years he is about 90. He isn't very active, in fact he is the ultimate couch potato. If you are lucky enough to be home with him your day will be filled with activity. Feed the dog, let the dog out, let the dog in, let the dog out, let the dog in, feed the dog, let the dog out, and let the dog in.

One day we discovered that we were letting the dog out many more times than usual and when he came back in he would drink all of the water in his dish and beg to be let out again. He became listless and weak, he was literally sicker than a dog. Through some careful diagnostic work we discovered he was diabetic. Now for the past 5 years, every morning Reggie will wag his tail and stand by his dish while we give him an insulin injection. He never complains because whenever he gets his insulin shot he gets to eat his breakfast. Sometimes he gets too much insulin and we find him collapsed on the floor and we have to revive him with some syrup. Occasionally he gets into garbage or finds some cookie crumbs left by the grandchildren and his sugar goes a bit too high so he gets some extra insulin later in the day. Either way Reggie is always the same; a friendly, loving dog accepting of anyone.

Reggie is showing his age now and I am sure the diabetes has helped speed the process. He has cataracts and can't see very well, he can't hear you when you call or whistle and he sleeps a lot. Returning home in the afternoon or evening you will find him stretched out on the floor in a deep sleep. He can't hear you approach so you can never really tell if he is still alive. We all know one of these times he will be resting in peace, but until then he will be the same friend to everyone, accepting and loving you no matter who you are or where you come from.

Mark Twain had an interesting way of describing life. "Heaven is attained by favor. If it were attained by merit you would stay out and your dog would go in." Maybe this world would be better off if we were all going to the dogs.

Best Friends

Lilyanne Hazel and Maddie her best friend

Killer Beets

I had convinced myself that I was dying. After spending two semi-sleepless nights wondering how the life insurance money would be spent and who would get my boat I finally confessed to my wife what was on my mind.

As a physician I am relatively good at being objective about someone else's concerns. Not when it comes to myself. There is an old proverb "When a physician treats himself, he has a fool for a patient." I now believe that. There is another saying that I like. The difference between major and minor surgery is simple. If it is on you it is minor, if it is on me it is major. I had convinced myself I had a major problem.

Fresh vegetables from the garden are supposed to be good for you. Raised organically there are no pesticides, herbicides or other chemicals to raise havoc with your internal organs. They provide vitamins, minerals, fiber all in a tasty package without unwanted calories. Just what your mother wants you to eat. They are healthy addition to any diet and highly recommended. Not beets.

A couple days after eating fresh beets I experienced what I thought was life threatening internal hemorrhage. This wasn't a trickle, it was the mother lode. Being a physician I decided to examine myself. I opened my shirt in front of the mirror and began probing. My six-pack abs had turned into a twelve-pack and now more closely resembled an old bag of marshmallows. I pushed, probed and palpated. No swelling. No pain. A bead of sweat broke out on my forehead and I felt slightly dizzy. "Oh great, now I am having a heart attack" I thought.

The last thing I wanted to do was needlessly worry my wife. She would have scheduled a colonoscopy for me before supper. I decided to wait a day or two before giving her the bad news. Instead I decided to tell a friend.

"Vell hey, dat's da vey it goes yah know. How's fishin'?" was the response I got back. I figured that he just wanted my tackle box and fishing rods.

I made it through work the first day without passing out. So far so good. Once the initial wave of panic subsided, I began to reason with myself and check off various possibilities in my mind. As each belch and gurgle passed without dire consequences I started to relax. I spent a fitful night, tossing and turning as I deliberated the statistical odds of survival.

I am not a hypochondriac. In fact I would lean much more to the side of ignoring my problems thinking they are normal and will resolve spontaneously. When you are starting down the back side of the hill in life, a little grunting, groaning and wheezing during the day is expected. If someone reports never having any problems I begin to wonder what they are on.

The next morning there was less "hemorrhage" and still no pain. Now the lack of pain began to concern me. At first I thought I had a bleeding ulcer and now I was convinced I had something much worse. If I was still alive tonight I would tell my wife.

That night I carefully explained the situation to my wife, not wanting to alarm her or cause undo concern. Her response was out of character. She displayed a total lack of compassion and nearly doubled over from laughing. She knew immediately that I was experiencing the side effects of beets but I knew they weren't just any beets, they were killer beets

Getting Clipped

My hair has been receiving less and less attention since I passed the landmark age of 50. Partly due to an increase in the relative space between hair follicles but also I have less interest in fussing with it. Hair has never really been a focus for me in the past anyway. Saturday mornings I don't bother combing because it is simply too much effort and no one is looking anyway. My wife looks out of necessity but she has become accustomed to my cosmetic indifference. When my children were at the impressionable ages of their early teens they would marvel at their mother's resilience. Arising each morning and having to look upon their beloved father day after day and still remain cheerful and focused was a good example of character building.

During my high school days my hair was much longer, extending all the way to my shoulders. That particular style ended abruptly on my enlistment into the U.S Army. Any efforts at regaining my former glory have been theoretical at best. Maybe it was that abrupt transition from hairy to hairless which served as a foundation for my distaste at getting haircuts. Perhaps it was the scissors slashing and snipping so close to my ears. I pitied the poor person given the task of making something acceptable out of the unruliness on the top of my head. Every person that has had the chance to cut my hair over the years has done an outstanding job without any advice from me. I never really wanted to be in the barber chair and so I haven't really taken an active interest in how it looked when I exited the chair. I would let them carve at will and I usually left intact and satisfied.

My wife is my greatest hair critic. She has concerns for my image but I doubt it is for my sake. She would rather be seen in public with a well coifed athletic type rather than a lumpy dumpy 50 something with hair that looks like an unraveled cotton ball. I don't mean to burst her bubble but with me at least, the retro look is out. Even if I wanted to, I could never return to long, thick, dark brown hair. I am stuck with bristly, patchy, gray and white stuff. She is a good sport and endures my indifference but one of her most frequently expressed comments is "You need a haircut!"

My response has always been logical, "I need a new fishing rod. I don't need a haircut. That is only an opinion." As usual we would compromise and I would concede to her domestic pressures. Scheduling haircuts is tricky. On days off I prefer to be hunting or fishing, on week days I have to work, during the noon hour I have to eat so that leaves the evening and night hours. March and August are about the only months I can fit a haircut into my schedule. Finding a friendly person to cut my hair between the hours of 9 and 11 PM is also difficult. It is with this dilemma that I have finally arrived at a solution to my hair styling.

Borrowing a hedge trimmer from my daughter's boyfriend I received my first domestic shearing. Actually it wasn't a hedge trimmer but may have been a pet clipper. Seated in a chair in the yard one of my children buzzed and clipped until there were drifts of prickly white hair on my shoulders and arms and all around on the ground. My hair, now too short to bend was unresponsive to my comb. I was satisfied. It was cheap and convenient. I wet it down and rubbed it with a towel. My hair stuck up all over and my head looked like a dandelion after the yellow was gone and the wind had blown away just a few of the tufts.

After the first amateur haircut my wife was ready to give a try. This time we bought a clipper set and she was ready to assert herself. Rather than forging ahead with confidence as my daughter had done, she paused, going through the various options and attachments.

"What are you doing, let's get started." I cautiously urged her on but careful not aggravate someone with a sharp object.

"Just hold on" she replied somewhat irritated by my impatience. "I am reading the directions first." My confidence level soared. If she were ever going to exact revenge for any of my past wrong doings, now would be the time. I held my tongue and listened to the clock on the wall.

"Well the attachments are kind of confusing but I understand the last item on the list."

"What does it say?" I asked gently, hoping for a stylish cut with minimal blood loss.

"Don't poke eyes!"

Source, clipartguide.com

Bird Brain

I am a firm believer in home maintenance as long I don't have to do it. It seems that we are barely settled in our house and already there are areas that need to be maintained and repaired. My wife reminds me that the carpet was put in before our youngest child was born. Now she thinks we need to upgrade before our youngest graduates from high school this spring. With any luck I might be able to hold off the carpeting issue for another year or two however I will have to address other needs.

If our carpeting is weathering the years well, our siding isn't. Living in the north woods we appreciate our environmental beauty and like to have our home blend in with the surroundings. The house is sided in cedar which is usually a good choice in our climate. It was a great choice until we were faced with the Asian beetle plague. Every little crack and space between the cedar planks on the side of our house became packed with little orange spotted bugs. As the bugs retreated into the cracks they were assaulted by woodpeckers.

One day last summer when leaving for work I stepped out of the front door and found pieces of our house lying on the sidewalk. Chips and chunks of the siding were falling from the second story. I looked up to see multiple holes drilled into the wall by super powered woodpeckers. For the next few days I worked at repairing the holes with nails, screws, putty and paint and then I figured out a great plan to foil those little feathered jack hammers.

That Saturday morning I went to the local sporting goods store and bought an owl decoy and a metal plant bracket. The plan was simple. I had no desire to shoot the feathered pests because I like to listen to them poking holes in my trees and chimney. Owls are a natural enemy of the woodpeckers so by hanging the great horned owl decoy outside of my second story bedroom window I would never again be awakened in the early morning hours by a pileated wrecking ball.

I climbed to the top of my ladder and bolted the metal bracket firmly in place near the area of greatest destruction. Once the bracket was attached to the siding I hung the owl decoy from a length of nylon cord. I was so sure of my plan that I spent the rest of the afternoon sitting in my lawn chair with a cold drink in hand waiting for unsuspecting woodpeckers to collapse from fright when they encountered the great horned owl of death. The rest of the day passed without any problems. I didn't see any woodpeckers dying from fright but I also didn't hear the familiar pecking and pounding on my house either. Problem solved.

It was somewhere after midnight when I heard the wind gather strength and change directions. I rolled over in bed and fluffed my pillow. As I yawned and tried to regain my fading dreams I heard a clunk on the side of the house. The first clunk was followed by another and then another. Not only was I awake now but my wife also was alarmed. This wasn't the gentle pecking of a little woodpecker, this was more like the neighbors throwing baseballs against the house, one after another. The rock hard great horned owl had come to life in the wind and was pulverizing the outside wall next to my head. With each gust of wind he swung like a wrecking ball on a cable against the side of the house whacking and cracking the hours away until in desperation I had to act.

Dressed for battle in a tee shirt, underwear and slippers I prepared for revenge on the great horned zombie that was pounding my house. At that hour my beloved wife wasn't going to come outside and hold the ladder so I had to devise another strategy. As I searched through my garage for ideas I was constantly interrupted by the staccato of the owl whacking my house. I came up with a plan of using an extension handle duct taped to a metal apple picker basket. The plan was to swing the 15 foot handle with the apple picker and catch the owl so I could break the cord and pull it down. In the strong wind it was like trying to hit a swinging piñata twenty feet in the air during a hurricane. I hoped the neighbors didn't wake up from the noise to see a deranged white haired man in his underwear flailing around outside.

My first attempts were weak and uncoordinated but finally I connected with a strong blow to the owl. This seemed to infuriate him and he flew even harder against the house so that my equally annoyed wife yelled out the window at me to "knock it off". I took that as encouragement to knock the owl off and I began swinging with more ferocity. Three or four more frantic blows later the owl finally succumbed to my attack and collapsed on the ground totally broken.

I returned to my bedroom and begged forgiveness at disrupting our night's sleep. She thanked me for being so brave as to face the world in my underwear. The wind died down and we returned to a comfortable sleep until the early morning hours. Sometime just after sunrise we were awakened to the gentle tap-tap of a woodpecker on the side of our house.

Skinny Legs

My family seems to be addicted to competition. Table games, hunting, fishing, fantasy football and even arguments must be finalized with a winner and a loser. Justice must always be served. I am willing to concede an argument in order to keep the peace but that doesn't always work. Winners must preside over losers.

Since we are deeply into our fantasy football season, matching wits, drafting players and battling it out on the gridiron it has become an easy process to extend our battles to other fields of play. One of our beloved children extended an invitation to compete in a family weight loss endeavor. No longer able to compete on wits and intimidation only, now I have to apply myself physically.

I received an invitation to register myself on "skinnyo.com". It is a confidential weigh in and then you enter your weight periodically over the time of the competition. I weighed in and prepared myself for the battle of the bulge. Youth and vitality is no match for old age and treachery.

Armed with secret medical information, I considered the competition unfair from the start. Beginning my preparation I pulled out old medical books and dusted off the diet and weight loss sections. Eat less, low fat, more exercise, Atkins, Ornish, Weight Watchers, Jenny Craig and countless other options were reviewed. Popular magazine headlines proudly touted how to "walk off belly fat". Other articles caught my attention. "How I Lost 40 pounds on the Chocolate Diet". How about "fat burner supplements" that would surely put me in front of the competition.

The truth is difficult to accept. When I get the urge to exercise, I usually lie down until it passes. I consider "diet" a four letter word. My four favorite food groups are pancakes, fried fish, apple pie and baked beans. It would be easier to sleep on the couch for a month than live without buffalo wings. So how could I possibly win the race? My wife is the secret ingredient.

She is disciplined and dedicated and she works overtime to keep me accountable. Fresh baked bread just out of the oven is a difficult temptation to overcome. Pulling two steaming whole wheat loaves from the oven, she allowed me to slice it but stood guard lest I slip a piece out of sight and coat it with butter when she turned her back. Accountability may be the key to success for most of us. Having someone to assist us in times of temptation or areas of weakness is a powerful reinforcement. I am thankful.

The contest is based on a percentage of weight loss over a period of time. The way I see it, if you don't have much to lose in the beginning, you can't win the contest. If you have more to lose at the start then you are sure to be one of the front runners. I can't help but feel I have the advantage.

My game plan calls for a varied approach. Not one to be stuck in a rut, I think that when I am around my accountability partner I will stick with the low fat, low calorie approach. On weekends when the football games are holding my attention I will switch to the Atkin's diet recommendations. Then when I am alone and free to choose anything I want, I will likely shift to the chocolate lover's weight loss plan. Exercise? Certainly. I should be able to burn most of my calories just shifting between the different diets. If that doesn't work then I can always fall back on treachery. I first weighed in while wearing heavy shoes and my keys in my pocket.

Over 50 Diet Plan

Eating is more than satisfying a lust for a certain food or curbing the pains of hunger. Dining is an adventure, diving into the mysteries of subtle flavors and aromas never before attempted. Every culture and country has their own unique style of preparing food. Hot and spicy, sweet and sour, bland, salty, boiled, fried, roasted or raw, food is meant to be enjoyed. Eating can also as simple as opening a package and inhaling without ever trying to discover the true origin of the contents. As I look back at my own culinary preferences I have progressed from the gulp and go method of eating to the more relaxed form of slow cooking and slow eating.

As a mere youth of 16 I could burn energy by just thinking. There were no caloric obstacles that could not be successfully surmounted. I remember the summer I first met the girl who would later become my wife. After 35 years of marriage she has remained about the same size; I haven't. One of our favorite hangouts was a small resort on the lake where we now live. The pinball machine was a dime, the hamburgers and pizzas were cheap and we could get their by walking. After a pleasant afternoon of doing whatever teenagers did in those days, we would stop by the resort for a snack. The juke box would sing out "The Night Chicago Died" while we played pinball and ate. I could eat a hamburger and a pizza and a couple of bottles of Mountain Dew as appetizers then we would go to her place for supper. Her mother was great cook so I never really stopped at one helping, and there was always dessert.

Most of the guys at that age were the same. Our insides were like Teflon. We could eat almost anything in huge amounts and it never seemed to stick. We could plow through food like a bulldozer and seldom reach our limit. Our preferences however seemed to lean toward quantity rather quality. When I graduated from High School I was finally up to a robust 145 pounds soaking wet. My, how times have changed.

A few years back I had the privilege of turning 50. I know 50 isn't really a miraculous milestone year but something changes at 50. After 50, what once leapt for joy now groaned and staggered a bit. Skin that was once taut is now stretched and sagged. Eyes that could see the finest details now demand glasses just to read the large print. Stomachs that could handle avalanches of greasy food washed down with syrupy drinks now revolt at the thought of anything spicier than oatmeal.

The general diet recommendations for anyone over 50 leave something to be desired. The first thing you need to do is taste your food. If it tastes good then you really shouldn't eat it. Elimination of salt is the next step. I like salt because it is salty. Why else would you eat it? Fat is the same. I hand out recommendations for low fat, low salt diets while munching on tortilla chips freshly fried in hot grease and doused in salt. (Do as I say, not as I do).

The real challenge to the over 50 crowd is the fiber issue. When I was 16 I thought fiber was something you used to make burlap sacks. After 50 we recommend fiber supplements that differ very little from ground up gunny sacks. Eating the gunny sack supplements often isn't enough so we mix it in prune juice and gulp it down. It is kind of like mixing some gun powder in a cup of gasoline. The effects can be explosive.

The perfect breakfast is now rather simple. Oatmeal with skim milk washed down with a prune juice-gunny sack shake. If your blood pressure isn't high you can have a cup of coffee. On the alternate days I have corn flakes. Only problem is corn flakes don't have enough fiber so I dump them out and eat the box. Occasionally in the evenings we may have a special meal allowing ourselves the luxury of a grilled steak or spicy fillet of salmon on the grill. Unfortunately we can't turn down the lights to enhance the romantic dining experience. Candles are banned. With all of the prune juice shakes, open flames are just too dangerous.

Bring Home the Bacon

The days when summer begins its slow descent from the hot, sultry nights into the cool mornings of early fall, I find myself in a happier mood. I love summer and all it has to offer but there is really something about fall that soothes my soul. I was born in September so that may be part of it. Apparently I didn't want to show myself until the maples were red and the sky was a deep blue. I love the smell of crunchy brown leaves underfoot and the crispness of the autumn air.

The fall season kicks off with one of my best holidays. One of my all-time favorite holidays is Ground Hog's Day. It officially marks the second of February which we all know is a red letter day. Equally important although less well known is International Bacon Day which occurs this year on September 3rd. Somehow Labor Day seems to get all the glory but International Bacon Day shouldn't be overlooked. It is somewhat like comparing Thanksgiving and Christmas. Christmas gets all of the glitter and glamor while Thanksgiving is often overlooked. We start hearing Christmas shopping advertisements shortly after International Bacon Day but we never hear about Thanksgiving until about the middle of November.

Actually I am glad these holidays aren't celebrated with shallowness and lack of feeling. That allows us true believers to celebrate these designated days for what they really mean. Thanksgiving isn't "Turkey day" but rather "Thanksgiving" day. It is a day to give thanks and to be thankful for all that we have. It is hard for Madison Avenue to sell you a bunch of junk when the focus is on being thankful and spending time with friends and family. Likewise International Bacon Day is about bacon and if you want to eat it with friends and family, that is up to you.

While you are preparing for International Bacon Day here are a few facts to help you get ready. Actually the smell of bacon is alluring. Bacon cologne was originally invented in 1920, in Paris by a butcher named John Fargginay. He discovered what we all know to be true today; bacon scent is more powerful than anything Calvin Klein can make up. Any woman should know that rubbing a bit of maple-cured, smoked pork fat on the neck can call their man from afar. No longer do you need to labor over "honey-do" lists and nagging. Simply rub it on and wave a bit of crispy side pork before his eyes and he will be putty in your hands. If you want to keep the magic alive then feed him bacon and eggs for breakfast, a BLT loaded with extra bacon at lunch and of course a bacon, double cheese burger at supper. Don't forget to eat healthy, so a salad with bacon bits never hurts either.

Bacon has become so important to us that we often take it for granted. It has become part of our day to day lives and we tend to overlook its significance. Each year in the US we eat about 2 billion pounds of bacon, most of it at breakfast. BLT's became popular when fresh fruits and vegetables were more available to the public. Before that we just ate bacon sandwiches. There are about 25000 people in the United States with the last name of Bacon, who couldn't love a name like that.

Bacon is also part of an idiom that signifies success. We may call the workers of the world "bread winners" but in truth we are more delighted when they "bring home the bacon". How many of us remember those provocative television ads for Enjoli perfume, with the woman singing how she can "bring home the bacon, fry it up in a pan and never, never let you forget you're a man". I don't know if this perfume is still available but it might have been more effective it actually contained essence of bacon. On International Bacon Day, make sure you bring home a greeting card and some bacon because if you ask your spouse "what's shakin' bacon" but you don't bring home the bacon, you won't be makin' bacon and then nothing is going to save your bacon.

Don't Make Me Think

I came home from work last week and something was different. It wasn't that I was later or earlier than usual but something just didn't seem the same. It is the strangest feeling when this happens when you sense something is new or changed or out of place but you really aren't sure. Then you begin to doubt if something really was changed or if you just think something changed. That particular day I just couldn't be sure.

At dinner time I looked uncomfortably around the room. Was the furniture moved? The room painted a new color? How about carpeting? New appliances? New dishes? I had a heightened sense of alertness that I normally didn't have after a long day of work. I didn't dare ask because if there wasn't anything new I didn't want to be perceived as being paranoid and if there was something new I didn't want to be viewed as being oblivious to the obvious. I chewed my dinner slowly as my eyes darted around the room. I would figure it out.

I cautiously tried the green Jell-O with pears. It tasted fine. I swallowed. I remembered she had been watching a true crime story on television a couple of nights past. The investigation and subsequent jury trial focused on a woman who had poisoned her husband with antifreeze mixed into green gelatin. Apparently her plan was successful because years later she tried the same thing with her second husband. I used the napkin to dab my brow. So far I was still husband number one.

"So how was your day dear?" I wondered silently if some small talk would bring out the plan or the change or whatever appeared to be so obviously different.

"Fine." She smiled back. No information, no clues. "More Jell-O?"

"Is it cold in here or is it just me?" I felt a shiver up the back of my neck.

"Don't worry, you won't freeze."

"I have been looking around the room and I have a feeling something is different. Did you make some changes in here...somewhere?" I pushed the bowl of green gelatin to the side as I watched her eyes. She flipped her hair back just a bit and reached for her glass.

"I didn't change anything in here. Why?"

"Well I was just thinking... something seems different, but I really can't be sure."

The evening progressed without event. My bubbling paranoia simmered down just a bit yet I continued thinking that I would soon discover the elusive but obvious difference in front of me. Then it hit me. It wasn't the house, it was her. There was something different about her, but what was it?

I avoided staring but would glance at her discreetly when she wasn't looking. Thinking couldn't reveal it and looking didn't find it either. I rested. Certain to discover the difference eventually, I went about my life as if nothing had changed. However, it wasn't until Sunday morning while greeting some friends that I was able to finally see things in a different light. Another woman causally walked up to her. "I like what you did with your hair."

"Hair?" I asked. "I thought there was something different about you!" There was no way to salvage my lack of sensitivity and inability to see the difference. Men can see the obvious color differences between a silver Ford truck and a silver Chevy truck. Men can hear the subtle differences between two different turkey calls. Men can taste the differences between 13 different barbecue sauces at a rib cook-off but don't expect a man to notice a haircut.

"Next time you cut your hair, warn me or put a sign out in the yard." I pleaded my case. "Just...don't make me think."

Inside the Hospital Gown (Part 1)

Rumors of my demise are greatly exaggerated, and of that I am well pleased. Regarding that incident I decided to use this forum to my advantage and set the record straight and also to convey to you lessons learned. Utilizing past experience can benefit the manner in which health care is delivered in the future.

This is how I recall the events of the past week, although others may have a different view. It was on a Monday and I was bracing myself for another busy day. I don't harbor a dismal view of Mondays as perhaps some do but rather look forward to the week. Casting off the cloak of a lazy weekend filled with fun and frolic, I was ready to face a new parade of disease and discomfort awaiting outside my office door. Having already met with two individuals to whom I offered my comfort and sage advice, I returned to my office and leaned upon my desk. Stricken with a bit of indigestion my face gave away my inward groaning and it was witnessed by my oldest daughter, the nurse practitioner.

"Are you alright" she inquired.

"I'm not sure" I responded "I have some chest pain." The moment those words escaped my lips I knew it was over.

The women of my family are not to be trifled with. They have been trained to be calm in crisis situations, act decisively and respond with courage. I also knew I had a responsibility to many beyond my immediate family to make sure that my "bit of indigestion" was nothing more serious. I willingly submitted myself to the barrage of poking and prodding that I have asked many of you to also undergo. It was a humbling experience, however through it I have gained a great deal of insight that I would not have otherwise fully understood.

Chest pain is not to be trifled with although many times it isn't due to a heart condition. Doctors and nurses could list numerous conditions that may cause chest pain. Most of them however, lack a true serious nature other than the fact that they may mimic a heart attack. However people don't die from indigestion, they die from heart attacks and therein lies the conundrum.

Upon my arrival to the emergency room I was ushered into the presence of the gate keeper. Disguised as a receptionist, she actually has power equal to most administrators. You see, she performs the most important procedure in health care, the wallet biopsy. With a deft movement and slight-of- hand that would rival a master pickpocket, she had my insurance card copied and recorded before I was able to mouth the words, "chest pain". Once I had satisfied the health care finance committee I next had to calm the lawyers. I responded to her request by recording my signature on the various disclosures, release forms and authorizations. Following those two most important initial steps I entered into the world of glaring lights and ice cold equipment. In a room where they have ways of making you speak and no secret goes untold. I was in the examination room.

A doctor and nurse converged at my bedside having dutifully dipped their hands and stethoscopes in ice water before entering. I felt the throbbing pulse radiate into my shoulder and neck as an automatic blood pressure cuff strangled my upper arm. A needle pierced a vein near my elbow on one side and near the wrist on the other. My precious O positive blood escaped into tubes and vials and was whisked away to waiting lab techs lurking behind heavy doors. There was no turning back now. I had arrived.

Inside the Hospital Gown (Part 2)

There comes a realization for most of us at some critical juncture of our lives when we finally understand and accept the tenuousness and fragility of human life. For some it may occur when they experience the loss of a loved one, for others it may be when they experience a sudden or serious health condition. For me it occurred when I forgot to make hotel reservations for our wedding night. I didn't learn from my mistake as I also forgot our first wedding anniversary. It was an educational event that left an indelible impression on me and is not to be forgotten.

Despite that early encounter with mortality, I am continually reminded of the preciousness of life. Almost daily we are exposed to serious health concerns or the loss of loved ones and we strive to offer wise compassionate advice and counsel. Yet in spite of our best efforts difficult problems arise. It was exactly this situation that I recently faced.

Chest pain should be considered cardiac in origin until proven otherwise. Often that can be determined by an examination as well as a review of the circumstances surrounding the onset of the chest pain. However most of the time it needs further testing. That is how I found myself inside the emergency room being evaluated for chest pain.

A critical part of the process has to do with the required uniform. All patients subjecting themselves to the inquiry of the doctor on call needs to have the proper attire. It really isn't something you wear but rather attempt to drape over the front of your body. It is nothing more than a cheap bed sheet with a couple of arm holes, a line of snaps and a string to tie around your neck. I have seen more style in a painter's drop cloth. It helps to remain seated while wearing the patient uniform because standing will certainly induce a draft on the back side.

Having donned the appropriate hospital approved clothing I was finally subjected to the necessary examination and testing. Blood testing was the easy part. A quick stab in the arm and it is off to the secret lab where they can tell if you have been eating bacon cheeseburgers and bratwurst for lunch every day. The EKG is a different matter.

The nurse with the ice cold hands was particularly relieved to find that she didn't have to shave my chest. I have never been blessed or cursed (depending on your point of view) with ample chest hair. Growing up without chest hair was always a source of manly embarrassment to me. Daily I would peer into the bathroom mirror trying to find just one hair to prove to myself that I wasn't a wimp. This went on for years. When I finally found one, it was already gray.

Pleased that she didn't have to waste precious time shaving my chest, she simply plucked the EKG wires out of the freezer and applied them to my shivering flesh. I did my best to stifle a gasp because I didn't want to induce a false reading of the electrical impulses emanating from my heart. Holding one's breath while under an icy assault is difficult but I relied on my past military training and I remained steadfast through adversity. The EKG tracing was satisfactory and I was permitted to begin breathing again.

Every health care organization makes a very serious effort to keep your health concerns top secret and this particular situation was no different. However, I being a member of the 6th generation of Ingalls to live in the Burnett County area posed a problem with secrecy. I had to be carted off through the hallway to the x-ray department while wearing the flimsy painter's drop cloth. Traversing the first 50 feet of hallway with the wind freely circulating around my anatomy I somehow managed to meet fellow coworkers, friends, administrators, strangers, colleagues, neighbors and former high school classmates in the hallway. A great time was had by all.

At the end of the day, my results satisfied the medical staff and I was sent home with instructions to return for the necessary "stress test" in two days. I would soon find out that the important part of that procedure isn't the test, but rather the stress.

Inside the Hospital Gown (Part 3)

Many adults have had the opportunity to subject themselves to a stress test. It is often performed at the recommendation of the physician because of symptoms reported or possibly due to a strong family history of heart disease. Regardless of the reason, it accomplishes a goal of challenging the persons physical stamina and more specifically the function of the heart.

A stress test can be performed in several different ways. The traditional and simplest way is to have the individual walk on a treadmill while monitoring the person's heart rate and blood pressure. The treadmill is programmed to increase in speed and change in elevation at predetermined times. The general idea is to drive you to the point of exhaustion so you are unable to talk back to the doctor. He or she can then lecture you without interruption about how fat you are and how much salt you eat and how you really should cut down on everything that tastes good.

There are several problems with the standard stress test. If works quite well if you want to determine someone's general level of fitness or endurance but it can be difficult to interpret at times. Sometimes the treadmill is combined with an injection of a radioactive medication to provide a more accurate assessment of the heart. If this is done on the treadmill you have to declare to the examiner when you have exactly one minute left before you are going to collapse. This can be tricky because if you are already on the verge of collapse, trying to mouth the words "I AM ALMOST DEAD NOW!" could go unnoticed and you will have to bravely continue your fight to survive another minute more than you planned.

A third option is the drug induced or chemical stress test. For the examiner this is actually easier because you are already in a prostrate position so CPR is easier to perform. Contrast that with the treadmill, where they have to pick you up off of the floor first to initiate the process of revival. Each of these options represent the "test" on your heart.

However, most health care providers fail to inform you of the first part of the equation; the "stress" part.

I had the benefit of having a drug induced nuclear stress test which meant I could not drink coffee on the morning of the procedure. Coffee is that vile, black, life-giving fluid most of us inhale shortly after awakening. Coffee is on the same level of importance as oxygen. On most days, coffee is more important than sex. Morning coffee is such a part of my life that I doubt I have missed a single day in 30 years, until my stress test.

After checking to make sure my life insurance was paid, my loving wife accompanied me on the 50 minute drive to the hospital. She cradled in her hands a supersized travel mug brimming with fresh brewed black coffee that she would slurp every few seconds. I sniffed the air and inwardly wept.

A nuclear stress test also requires a nuclear scan. This means the nurse will start an IV and then you have to go and sit in the waiting room next to the coffee pot for an hour. Following that you are escorted into a locked chamber and the truth serum arrives in a container that actually looks like a lead lined beer stein. Following the injection of the radioactive beer stein medication you are perched on a narrow bed with two large white panels surrounding your body. You have to remain as motionless as possible for the duration of the test with your arms above your head. Laughing, crying, burping and dreaming of coffee are strictly forbidden. I was most fortunate to have survived the 20 minute nuclear interrogation only to find out that the equipment malfunctioned. Another wait by the coffee maker and another scan while lying in suspended animation.

The last part of the stress test is the actual procedure. Lying on a different bed with frigid wires attached to your chest and legs you are instructed to just relax. HA!! I made the critical mistake of reading about the test on the internet. Relax??? After digesting the various personal experiences posted on "Google" I knew I was going to die.

The nurse injected another vial of truth serum into my veins and it happened. My heart rate doubled and an elephant jumped out from behind the curtain and did a dance on my chest. I felt the cold grip of death grasping at my ankles trying to drag me under. I tried to breathe deep and slow, attempting to shut out the blackness that was soon to shroud my soul. And then it was over.

The headache and chest pressure subsided just as they said it would. The IV was removed and the wires unclipped. Another quick scan in the secret room and I finally gulped my first cup of coffee for the day. I had survived. I am happy to report to all concerned that my heart remains in normal working condition without any problems.

My experience is worth passing on. Chest pain is nothing to be ignored. It is far better to undergo the necessary testing and find out that everything is ok rather than ignoring the situation and discovering that you are now in a serious or life threatening condition. If you are having symptoms of unusual trouble breathing, or chest pain or pressure make sure you get this evaluated. Just as Benjamin Franklin once said, "An ounce of prevention is worth a pound of cure."

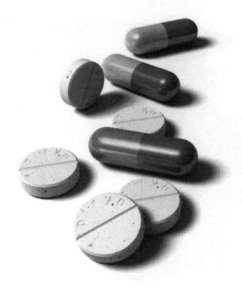

Medical Malapropism

Communication with your doctor is difficult enough when you have to explain vague symptoms about internal systems you don't really understand. Throw in a dash of modesty and a few big words and you have a recipe for confusion or certainly a setting for misunderstanding. Physicians struggling with overloaded schedules often leave uninformed and sometimes embarrassed patients to grasp at words when describing their symptoms. Often those confusing to understand and difficult to pronounce words are blurted out with a passing hope of connecting with the doctor or nurse practitioner.

"I am having trouble with my psychotic nerve." One individual admitted.

I sat back to assess their mental stability. " Are you feeling some stress or problems at home?" I asked, trying to gently bring out the basis for their concern. Not wanting to offend or appear judgmental I probed further. "What do you think is the problem?"

"Well ever since I raked the yard I have been having problems." Now I thought I was getting somewhere.

"You don't like raking the yard, is that right and it is getting on your nerves?" I followed up expecting an affirmative reply.

"No you dolt! It is my psychotic nerve. I have a pain in my butt from my psychotic nerve." It was now clear to me. Our conversation had struggled because we were victims of a medical malapropism syndrome, the misspoken medical word. Sciatic nerve and psychotic nerve have the same meaning if you don't know the definition of either one. Medical practitioners have to be on their toes to clearly understand the concern of the hurting patient.

Another and possibly the most common malapropism has to do with the male anatomy. "Doc, I got prostrate troubles."

"Do you have problems when you are lying down?" "Oh yeah, mostly at night, I have to get up three or four times to go to the bathroom." Of course I know someone is actually talking about their prostate and not about lying prostrate but similar sounding words are often substituted innocently. I suppose someone could become psychotic from their sciatic nerve or one's prostate may in fact make them prostrate.

Perhaps the most humorous and potentially embarrassing malapropism occurred very innocently during a routine visit. A young woman had presented for a routine examination. After discussing a variety of health topics and answering her questions I motioned for her to take a seat on the examination table. After checking her ears and throat I applied my stethoscope to her chest to listen to her heart and lungs. After listening to her heart sounds I instructed her breath deeply.

"Big breathes" I said.

She hesitated for a moment and then replied, "Thankth"

Driving in the Fog

I sympathize with the newest generation entering the work force. Uncertain political and economic times is unsettling enough for those of us who have made a mark in the world but it is doubly so for those just graduating. The educational process is great at developing the intellectual mindset but I have always felt it lacks true credibility at preparing one for the actual process of working.

One of our delightful offspring is struggling with career decisions. She isn't afraid of work and she has a good work ethic but there remains a serious and persistent level of anxiety about her entry into the work force. Uncertainty plays a role in this but perhaps we have failed her as well. Many children see their parents as stable and settled as if they had it all together. I am sure some young people can't believe their own parents were once awkward teens harboring the same insecurities they now have. After all haven't all parents always known exactly what they were going to do in life and everything turned out exactly as planned?

My advice is easy but incredibly difficult to follow. Go for a drive on a foggy day. I have often related to each of our children that life is actually a bit like driving in the fog. You start out with a general knowledge of where you want to go but you make a thousand adjustments in the process. Only able to see just so far it is easy to become anxious when thinking about the final destination but that also is what makes it so interesting. Those twists and turns in the road and the detours along the way lead us to so many unplanned and expected joys that we never would have encountered if we had lived out the boring path we had planned.

My own life is an example. Born during that prosperous post war time I am part of a generation known as the baby boomers. The oldest members of this generation are now retiring and the youngest members are just beginning to figure things out. You see we were a free spirited group of people that changed politics and the work place. We grew up during tumultuous times of the Vietnam War, long hair, psychedelic colors and the Beatles. For many, life wasn't just driving in the fog, we lived in the fog.

My point being, having our lives planned out just never really occurred to most of us. I planned to get out of high school and become a Mountain Man like Jeremiah Johnson. While making plans to head to the mountains I ended up joining the U.S. Army as a way to get there. Colorado was my home for 3 years but I found that I missed the lakes and woods of northern Wisconsin. My wife's educational efforts then lead us to Northern MN where I worked as a restaurant assistant manager. At least that was my title but I actually spent most of my time chopping lettuce and grilling steaks for others.

Going to medical school wasn't even considered. Living my life in the fog I was destined to make many adjustments on my road in life. Never quite satisfied with my status quo I was forever searching. I was never certain about that for which I was searching but I kept looking anyway. Along the way I cleaned chimneys, cut brush on the roadways, cleaned milk trucks at Burnett Dairy, worked for Johnson Lumber delivering sheetrock and shingles, was a traveling bird feeder salesman, insulated chicken houses and attics, and did field work for a farmer. We even had our hand at homesteading where we raised our own vegetables, chickens, ducks, pigs and cattle.

Reflecting back, I am glad I never really had it all figured out. I am happy for all of the young people now considering their future positions in this world. It is comforting to know many of them have it all written down and cast in stone. I am surprised at the turns my life has taken. I went places and did things I would never have considered possible and not because I planned it out. One day I just started driving in the fog and found out that I really enjoyed the ride.

Remote Control

On May 22, 2012, Mr. Eugene J. Polley passed away from natural causes. He was 96 years old. While most of us don't know Mr. Polley, we are all familiar with what he developed. As an engineer working for Zenith he invented the television remote control device which is a precursor to our current multifunctional remote control devices. The family has announced that, following the football season, his ashes will be scattered between the couch cushions.

The original remote control was actually a small control device directly connected to the television by wires. While functional, it caused numerous problems as people were tripping over the wires. That particular remote control was actually named "Lazy-Bone". Mr. Polley took this concept and developed a control device that operated on flashes of light. Different triggers or buttons would transmit different flashes of light that would be picked up by photo cells located on corners of the TV. If you wanted to adjust the volume you simply pointed the control at the correct corner of the television and pulled the trigger on the gun shaped control. He named his version "Flash-Matic" based on the method of operation.

Remote controls today operate on infrared signals. You can play games with it by trying to adjust your television by bouncing the signal off of windows, mirrors or any reflective surface. It becomes more challenging if you try to bounce the signal off of two or more surfaces at the same time, much like a two rail shot in billiards.

There may be future benefits of remote controls which are yet to be developed although we are now on the cusp of discovery and implementation. Currently you can use a smart phone to adjust your furnace, turn on or off lights and even program your DVR to record television programs, all from a distant location. You can also access your bank accounts and pay bills, transfer money and monitor retirement accounts or other investments. While not utilizing the same technology, it still remains a form of remote control. However the real benefit will be realized when we can utilize a remote to control our children or spouse or coworkers. Who wouldn't love to hit the fast forward button when the boss is rambling on through an intensely boring meeting or the mute button when your spouse reminds you for the 47th time of something about which you no longer want to be reminded.

How about your children? Too loud? Hit mute. Too rambunctious? Push the pause button or the slow motion button. Husband coming home from work late again? Try the search button. Perhaps the ease at which we may control others would also cause us a fit of frustration as others would use the same measures upon us.

I have found a recent situation that is somewhat related to the above scenarios. My father recently acquired a set of hearing aids. Now with the latest technology he is able to enjoy the finest in television viewing without bothering his fellow viewers. Others in the room can adjust the television volume to their comfort level and he then adjusts his hearing aids to the volume that satisfies him. Technology to the rescue. Ironically he adjusts the hearing aid volume control not with a tiny twist button but rather with a remote control. That's right, he picks up a small remote control device not unlike the one used to adjust his television and points it at his head. A quick press on the correct button and he is satisfied.

Ironically my mother has found another use for the device. When she wants to talk about something that she would rather keep confidential, at least from dad, she secretly wields the remote control. A sly point and press the button and he has no idea what she said. Now that is a functional remote control.

Pain Scale

For those of you have been following my latest adventure you may be aware that I have just survived a back surgery. Reaching the decision to do this was relatively easy, I was miserable. The surgeon said I needed it and I said "ok". Having the surgery was easy, the next day provided a different perspective.

In the medical field we try to quantify subjective complaints. In other words we try to take symptoms that are hard to judge and apply numbers to the level of discomfort. This is a way for us to judge if we are actually making progress in managing pain. Most of you with pain have been exposed the simple 1...10 pain scale. 1 is no pain and has a cherubic smiley face beside it. 10 is the worst pain you can imagine and has a grumpy face next to it. The problem with this scale becomes apparent after you have suffered in pain. I suspect this was developed by someone in a shiny suit in a pleasant office after a nice long relaxing lunch. It was not developed by someone who was suffering.

If the doctor or nurse asks you how bad your pain is and you say an 8 that should mean it is quite bad. But what if the next time it is worse, is it now a 9 or 10? The scale only goes up to 10. When asked about pain in these situations the number is now often 15 or 20. After you have had back surgery the numbers change largely because there is an emotional component to the pain. I now know what it is like to scream in pain during the night when your body is paralyzed by the spasms in your back and you need help to simply shift your position in bed. You ask for more pain pills realizing that they only take the edge off of the pain while turning your insides to cement. On a scale of 1 to 10, at that moment it was off the chart. Pain is very subjective and hard to explain.

I think the pain scale should be modified. Instead of a smiley face progressing to a grumpy face or a scale of 1...10 we should perhaps qualify the pain in the way we express pain to our family and friends. "Not Bad" is a good starting point. Not bad or pretty good are reasonable ways of saying there may be some discomfort but I can handle it. After that everything is basically bad but in varying degrees. Unlike the existing pain scale that stops at a grumpy face and "10" there is nothing worse than the worst description on my pain scale.

Not Bad...Annoying...Miserable...Terrible...$#@%&#$...JUST PUT ME OUT OF MY MISERY. A pain scale such as this actually expresses the way we think and feel. When you are in pain I don't know what a 7 or 8 means but I do know what "$#@%#$" means and so does everyone else. Annoying may become Miserable with time or we may have episodes of "not bad" but no one wants to be at the end. It isn't a 9 or 10 or even 1000. I have seen people in this condition and although I have never had pain this severe I know it exists.

I have learned some lessons in all of this. Doctors suffer just like anyone else. We put our pants on the same way and we share the same anxieties and pains. I know what it is like to lie naked on a cold surgical table while strangers scrub your skin and put purple lines where they are planning to cut when you are helpless. I know what it is like to be confused and drugged from the medications. I know what it is like to be incapacitated and require assistance with the simplest tasks. I also know what it is like to do the exercises and work through the pain and get better.

I have learned that I don't have all of the answers but I do understand someone just a bit better because of what I have gone through. When someone comes to me and is worried or in pain; I can understand. When someone can't put their own socks on, I know because I have been there. I have also learned to trust the advice and direction of the doctors and nurses entrusted with my care.

I have been somewhat amused by the descriptive designations for the severity or invasiveness of surgeries. But now I have also learned the difference between major surgery and minor surgery. Whatever the procedure might be, if it is on you it is "Minor" and if the surgery is on me then it is "Major".

The Name Game

Names are a title that we carry with us from beginning to end. I realize that some go to extra effort to change their given names from whatever was assigned by their parents but most just accept it and get on with life. It may represent something from your family or ethnic heritage or it may be something original but your given name meant something to your parents.

Names of ethnic origin may be traditional or perhaps borrowed from a hero or heroine. Thor for example is of a name of Scandinavian origin and conjures up an image of strength and power. Zeus is another name of Greek mythology that has substance. I prefer traditional names exactly for that reason; substance. I struggle with modified designer names.

Do any of you remember the children of musician, Frank Zappa? Dweezil, Diva, Ahmet and Moon Unit Zappa clearly had designer names. I am sure the names meant something to dear old mom and dad but how did the children feel? It's like the famous Johnny Cash song, "A Boy Named Sue". I was told of a mother of twin boys that actually named her children, "Oranjello" and "Lemonjello". That was different but it meant something to the mom. They were her favorite gelatin flavors.

Some parents name their child a traditional name but change the spelling to make it unique. Fred becomes Phred, Jennifer is changed to Gynnipher, Larry morphs into Lairee and Bob remains Bob. Actually changing the spelling of a name can sometimes be a positive factor. Most people know about Oprah, the world class entertainer and business woman. What many don't realize is that she originally was meant to be named Orpah, after a woman identified in the Old Testament. A simple unintended transposition of two letters is now synonymous with fame and fortune.

Regardless of traditional or designer names it still has meaning to the bearer. We all like to hear our name associated with something of lasting value or character. Sometimes we discover something and it is named in honor of the discoverer. America is named after Amerigo Vespucci, the straits of Magellan are of course named after famed explorer, Magellan and Johnson Lake is named after someone named Johnson.

What about anatomical names. We think all of our body parts as being derived from Greek or Latin origins but actually numerous areas are named after the person who first discovered it or described it. Most people are aware of Achilles tendon or Adams apple but what about the circle of Willis or Lovibond's angle? Many aren't aware of the ligaments of Cooper until they start to stretch then they are known as Coopers droopers.

Sometimes it isn't a body part that is named but rather it is a space or opening. I can only imagine someone poking around in a body and they discover a hole. Perhaps that is how the space of Disse or the epiploic foramen of Winslow was named. Have you ever heard about Rathke's pouch, the canal of Schelmm or the sphincter of Oddi?

We are acquainted with these areas but never really know the names. Young couples planning a family may notice an acceleration of the bundle of His when the Raphe of Holzer gets within close proximity to Grafenberg's spot or the recesses of Mulvey. Fillopio's tubes are certain to play a role in the process and after the baby is born you can cut through Warton's jelly.

What's in a name? Everything. Expectant parents, when you are pondering potential names for your offspring give them a good name, a name they can be proud of because you can never be too certain that we won't have one of our body parts with their name attached. No one wants to hear from their physician that their "Moon Unit" doesn't work properly. How much more distinguished it is to discover that your Crypts of Lieberkuhn or Kiesselbach's Plexus has fallen on hard times. Give them a name we can all wear proudly.

Don't Blink

I just returned from saying goodbye to a friend. She was 91 years old when she decided to go home. Of course I didn't know her for the entire 91 years of her life but I did know her for a moment, a blink in time. I thought back over the past few years and how this moment has been repeated in much the same way; you blink once and you wonder what happened, you blink twice and you're gone.

It seems that the world around us is racing past in a blur. Nowhere is it more apparent than when raising children. I remember the day we brought our oldest child home for the first time. Like most first time parents we had harbored some uncertainties about our knowledge and abilities but in retrospect it didn't really matter. For the first week we counted every burp and gurgle she made. The second week she went to kindergarten and the third week she asked for the car keys. We blinked and she was married.

With each of our children it was same. They went from potty training to prom in a matter of days. Life goes by at such a rapid pace that it takes a very clear mind to be able to keep it all straight. One evening I was looking through some family photos. Studying some of the individual photos of our girls I chose one in particular and brought it to my wife.

"Look at this picture. If you cover up the hair and the face and just look at the eyes it looks just like Anna (our second daughter)."

She rolled her own eyes in disbelief. "That is Anna!"

"You're kidding me! Well who are these other kids?" I blinked and stared at the young women seated around the table. "Who are you?"

I am amazed at how the ravages of time have affected those around me but yet I remain unaffected. I was a scrawny 145 pound dark haired kid when I met the girl who would be my wife. I haven't changed a bit. It seems like we were married just a couple of years and suddenly we had grandchildren. Now each morning when I look in the mirror I wonder what happened. The skinny dark haired kid is gone and staring back at me is a chunky white haired gnome with bags under his eyes. Each morning I try to slick down the spiky white hair as I rub the sleep out of my eyes. I blinked and I changed.

I am both happy and frustrated with my wife. I keep blinking and she never changes. I am also humbled when absolute strangers introduce themselves to me and ask me if the young woman at my side is my daughter.

One summer we were in the middle of a remodeling project in our home. Contractor and crew members gathered around the work site discussing the situation. It was clear that they needed my input on the decision making process. The crew boss walked up to our front step and rang the doorbell.

It was a Saturday morning. I was somewhere out of sight relaxing with my second cup of coffee. My wife answered the door, barefoot in a baggy sweat shirt and jeans.

"Can I help you?" she probably flipped her hair back out of her face.

I heard the worker stammer just a bit. "Uh…Is your dad home?"

Confident and proud she simply stepped away from the door and turned in my direction. "Dad there's someone here to see you!" She smiled, I blinked.

A Sundae Drive

Ever since the first Model T Ford rolled off the assembly line Americans have had an infatuation with their cars. Most of us recall names such as Buick or Packard or maybe even Pierce Arrow but what about Duisenberg, LaSalle, Hudson, Nash or DeSoto? As the classic cars of the 1930's and 1940's faded away the muscle cars of the 50's and 60's made their appearance. The Ford Mustang or the classic '55 Chevy now carry hefty price tags and are pampered and polished by their owners.

No longer was the automobile simply used for transportation or commuting. It became a focal point in society as entertainment and dining became connected with the family car. The first drive-in theater opened in 1933 and the first Sonic drive-in which promoted the automobile dining experience, opened in 1953 in Oklahoma City, serving hamburgers, hot dogs and root beer. Sonic now has over 3500 drive-in restaurants across the country. Recognizing this success many independent drive-in eateries were started and continue to thrive in small towns across America.

It was one of these classic American eating establishments which became our destination on Sunday. I can't say that I have a love affair with my car. Not anywhere near new and certainly not a classic, it is functional and paid for so there is little incentive to change. After attending church services on Sunday we turned the car toward the local drive-in and settled into a stall.

The car hops were quick to attend to our nutritional wants and needs. After surveying the menu posted on the sign we ordered and waited. Most cars today have power windows, even older cars, so before we gave our menu selections we had to turn on the car key.

It was perhaps a slightly longer wait than usual but not to any significant degree. The food was served hot and tasty. A classic cheese burger and fries and a frosty mug of root beer was my selection and a great way to begin the seasonal drive-in dining experience. I slurped the icy root beer, savoring the syrupy sweetness. We talked, we laughed and we visited with other diners enjoying the same experience. It was relaxing and a great way to spend some lazy time on a Sunday afternoon.

After licking the last bit of salt from the French fries off of our fingers one the passengers in the car decided to order a vanilla shake. Another order and another short wait but we had no plans and no need to hurry off. Finally it was time to leave. Most diners signal their plans for departure by starting the car. I turned the key but there was no surge of the engine only a sickly anemic clicking sound from the starter. The dome lights flickered and faded. In disbelief I turned the key again and again only to hear the same clicking. It seemed to be sending out a Morse code signal to anyone within hearing distance that there was an idiot behind the wheel. The clicking faded into an electronic groan and then silence. The battery was dead.

One of the other diners at the Drive-in graciously agreed to drive to our home and get a pair of jumper cables. (He had no choice in the matter, he was our son-in-law). Since we weren't going anywhere, we ordered again. This time it was a chocolate banana shake and a crème-di-mint sundae. We talked and laughed at our predicament. Frankly it was very relaxing to be stranded at a place where we could continue eating as long as we wanted.

Eventually we were rescued. A simple connection of the cables and we were headed down the road none the worse for being stranded. We actually learned a simple lesson. If you want to recharge your batteries, go for a sundae drive.

Bargain Bungalow

Lodging for the casual traveler can be a challenge. Business travelers may have the benefit of travel agents and prearranged business conferences so their options are usually above average quality. Not so the budget traveler. Seeking to save a few bucks on your lodging can help offset food and fuel expenses. Bargain offers may often seem like a good deal until the weary traveler arrives at their dream destination only to find out the photos in the brochure were taken years ago and the idyllic wilderness setting has turned into a landfill. Well intentioned cost cutting can be detrimental to your holiday bliss.

I have had the privilege of staying at some very nice locations, however usually at a nice price. I have nothing against paying for quality. I generally prefer to shop for quality products realizing that in the long run it is often the least expensive. That isn't always the case with holiday travel plans. However, you may get better vacation memories with a cheap destination, but you need to let your cheap destination memories sort of gel for a few years before you bring them out for review. If you try to relive those experiences too quickly you may be met with scowls, anger or even threats of violence.

On our wedding night I forgot to make reservations at any place. I never considered it necessary. I figured we would just drive blissfully off into Vacationland and stay where ever our little hearts desired. Holding hands as we drove away, we blissfully looked into each other's eyes pledging our undying love for eternity. By 10:30 that night the hand holding had turned into a white knuckle death grip and our eyes no longer met. Her eyes red from crying and probably pent up anger and mine red from driving for hours, we tried to stare ahead into the dark highway hoping for vacancy signs. After turning down offers for loaned tents along the highway we finally found our love nest. The exorbitant sum of $37.50 per night was paid and we enjoyed the polka dot burlap lamp shades and worn shag carpet. It was a memory that keeps on giving.

Realizing what great memories my past cheapskate decisions have made, I decided to continue the tradition. We had booked a trip to the Caribbean which required an overnight stay in Miami. Scheduled to arrive late and leave sometime the next day, I could see no reason to pay for anything other than a bed and a door that you could secure. The photos on the internet looked inviting with the swaying palms, aqua blue pool filled with laughing guests, tropical drinks in hand.

Landing in Miami was a shock to our winterized bodies. Sweating with our bags we finally found a hotel shuttle that went to that part of town. All of the other shuttles came and went several times to the nearby brand name places. I could see my traveling companions' white knuckle death grip on their luggage as we left behind the English speaking world and plunged into the side streets of Miami, Florida. I had no fear as I have a solid grasp on rudimentary Spanish for the traveler. I could say "please"," thank you" and "where is the bathroom" fluently. Our driver said something in Spanish and smiled. I nodded affirmatively although I had no idea what he said. We arrived on the narrow street with the blinking neon sign.

The fact that they didn't accept credit cards should have been a warning to us but when you are nearing midnight it didn't register very well. I watched the guest in front of us pay with a large roll of cash from his pocket. My wimpy wad of twenties seemed rather anemic but I had no desire to start a contest. We paid cash and lugged our bags up the narrow creaking stairs. Once inside I secured the door with the three available locks and we took stock of our surroundings.

The bed sheets were clean and white. That's all we could add to the positive list. On the negative side we found the phone ripped out of the wall with a large hole remaining in its absence. My daughter thought she found bullet holes in the wall near her bed but I tried to reassure her that it could have been caused by other projectiles as well. The bathroom had a large gap around the floor and wall into which you could lose personal items and never recover them. The normal humid and damp environment of tropical locations didn't help the odor either. We couldn't be sure that armies of spiders and cockroaches didn't reside in the depths of the walls, using the gaping holes in the walls as a refuge until they resurface under cover of darkness. With each twitch and itch during the sweaty night we resisted the urge to turn on the bare light bulb hanging above the bed and start swatting the imaginary bugs crawling across our bodies. If the imaginary insect population didn't kill us we were equally certain that the Miami police would find our bodies mugged and drugged somewhere in a dumpster.

Morning found us red eyed and weary but alive. My wife and daughter insisted we depart in a taxi before the bed sheets had cooled, bypassing the complimentary coffee in the dark smoke stained room that passed for a lobby. Realizing that our return travels would require another one night stay in Miami the following week I offered to make reservations before leaving. I was out voted and we had to stay in a place that accepted credit cards. I may have saved a couple of dollars but the memories were priceless.

Becoming a Medical Jargonaut

Preparing for a visit with a physician can be intimidating especially if it involves a new visit with a specialist. It may involve inconvenient scheduling and confusing travel instructions in another city. It could also include an in depth interview for a complicated problem. Prior to the visit you may have also received a history form where you can describe your affliction in details that you don't normally consider. In addition to all of that you may have many questions and sometimes these go unasked or unanswered because you may feel intimidated.

Don't fear going to the doctor. He or she is just like everyone else. We have the same fears and worries and we get afflicted with the same illnesses and injuries as anyone else. We may know the healthy choices but we don't always make them. Doctors may have huge amounts of education that the general public doesn't have but that doesn't always heed our own advice. The big difference between doctors and patients is the fact that doctors know and use big words that most other people don't know.

Learning a few of those big words before going to the doctor may be helpful in trying to understand your affliction. Memorizing a few medical words may help you impress your friends at dinner parties or late night trivia games but actually learning the prefixes and roots and endings will help you make up your own medical words. No need to spend 15 years of intense study, in a very short time you too can practice medical jargon on your own family.

The first word to learn is generic although it really isn't a big word and technically it isn't a medical word. Generic is important if you are concerned about cost. Doctors only use the word generic when talking about drugs. We don't like to talk about generic illnesses. Generic illnesses are problems that most people acquire at some time in their lives. If you come into the office with a stuffy nose, perhaps a low grade fever and a cough you might think you have a cold. A cold is a generic illness and if we call it a cold we can't charge as much. The proper terminology is viral rhinitis. If it is a bad cold we might call it a viral mucopurulent rhinosinusitis. You don't want to tell your friends and family that you went to the doctor for just a cold so learn the big doctor words and impress them. It may be enough to get you some extra sympathy and a day off work. If you don't have insurance or you have a large deductible then it is worth asking about generic illnesses. They tend to be cheaper but not always. Brand name diseases are usually much more expensive and serious, especially if the disease happens to be named after you personally.

Rash is another generic medical word you should try to avoid. We all know a rash when we have it but you should learn the proper word which is dermatitis. Dermatitis means inflammation of the skin. You can then add important descriptive words to make the rash more virulent if necessary. A raised itchy rash becomes a "generalized pruritic maculopapular cutaneous eruption". If it only itches for a short time we say it is "self limiting" but if you have a 7 year itch we would call that a "Perennial Pruritic Personal Problem". See how easy it is.

Next learn some of the suffixes or word endings. Something-ectomy means to cut out something such as an appendectomy (removal of appendix). Something-ostomy means to make an opening such as colostomy. Something-otomy means to make a surgical opening and just look around, then close it up. An example of this would be a laparotomy where the surgeon makes an incision in the abdomen to fix something internally. Usually these get combined. You likely would have a laparotomy to have an -ectomy and you could end up with an -ostomy. Be sure to read the fine print before you sign on the dotted line.

There is one other word worth knowing, idiopathic. It is one of the most important and most frequently used medical words. If you break the word apart it can help you understand the actual meaning. Pathos is Greek for disease or suffering from which we get the word pathology or the suffix –pathy or –pathic. Idio- is the tricky part because it means "one's self or within" but in actual use it means "without knowing" because we don't know. If we don't know, we say it came from within (such as it's all in your head). Idio- is also the root word for idiot. However just because your doctor may not know the reason you are suffering, it doesn't imply that he or she is an idiot and saying idiopathic doesn't imply that you are an idiot either.

Now when the doctor says you have an idiopathic maculopapular dermatitis combined with a mucopurulent rhinosinusitis you can just relax. Based on your extensive medical knowledge, you will already know that you have a common cold and a rash. Just have some chicken noodle soup, take two aspirins and in a few days you will feel better.

Back When I was a Kid

Memories of our childhood are filtered through time, enough to take the edge off of the worst times and make the good years into the best of our lives. Now when trying to put a current issue into perspective for my own children I find myself comparing their lives to the life I lived as a child. With the rapid changes occurring in our society, a few years can bring about changes that astound us. One thing that actually remains timeless is the way parents like to use the phrase "Back when I was a kid...".

Back when I was a kid... I cringed when I heard myself use the very words my father and grandfather used ... back when I was a kid. How often have we heard about walking to school in the middle of winter. It was 10 miles at least and uphill both ways and always 20 degrees below zero. Back when I was a kid, it was different.

I marvel at how things have changed in my lifetime. Clothing is a simple example. Microfiber fleece clothing is so soft, warm and comfortable it is hard to imagine winter with out it. My favorite relaxing-at-home shirt is a fleece pullover that feels instantly warm when I put it on. Back when I was a kid...there I go again. There was cotton and wool. Yes it was warm if you had enough layers on, but the wool made you itch like you had fleas and the wool coat was so heavy it felt like the sheep was still in it. Winter boots today are so vastly superior to anything we used to have. Black five-buckle overshoes slipped over plastic bread bags that were pulled over your street shoes were the common winter footwear. Sometimes you even added a few layers of newspaper in the bottom of the overshoes for insulation. If the boots leaked, you didn't throw them out and buy new ones. They were patched with a typical tire or inner tube patch. If you were a middle child, your boots often had two or more patches and then you usually used two bread bags on your feet for good measure. The poor kid's, whose mother baked bread at home, had to go without bread bags on their feet.

Winter clothing may have changed but nothing like telephones have changed. I recently bought a new cell phone after I lost mine in the bottom of the lake. I wanted something I could just talk into. You can't get that anymore. Cell phones are amazing. You can take pictures, video, check the stock market, watch a football game, check email and even talk to people on the new phones. Most people who have these don't actually talk to people they "text". It has become a personal, portable, portal for social networking. Back when I was a kid... we had a rotary dial phone on a party line. That was the social networking device back then. When someone else was called, you listened. You would never lose your phone because it was always attached to the wall. We didn't have to be in touch with everyone in the world every minute of our lives. It was kind of nice not being available.

Health care is something that has changed dramatically. Back when I was a kid going to the Dr was a big event. You didn't go for colds, flu, poison ivy or wood ticks, maybe you would go if you had a bad laceration or something more serious. You generally stayed home and if you survived the home remedies then you could go back to school or work. Home remedies generally included hot soup, Watkins liniment and vick's vaporub. When you went back to school everyone knew you had been sick because they could smell you coming before you walked in the door. Going to the Dr when you were sick often meant getting a penicillin shot in the butt.

I want to believe that life is better now compared to "back when I was a kid" but I am not so sure. I am utterly amazed at how complicated we have made our world. I am very thankful for the opportunity to have grown up in a much simpler time even though it really wasn't that long ago. That reminds me, have I ever told you about the way it used to be "back when I was a kid...?"

Highway to Heaven

Traveling in a foreign country can be a challenging. Mentally there is the stress of misunderstanding the language or directions and getting completely lost. Buses and trains arrive and depart quickly, flashing their route or destination in foreign languages allowing only a moments notice and a quick decision to jump aboard or wait for the next ride. Physically there is the risk of sudden death at the hands of a crazed taxi driver speeding through red traffic lights and busy intersections in an attempt to get a better tip from his American passengers. In my personal experience, foreign travel has the emotional impact of extreme sports and risky behavior that brings you to the edge of your chair wondering if you will ever have a second chance at anything. Thankfully I have never been in a serious accident overseas, although on one occasion I thought I had a brief but memorable view of the afterlife.

Mexico is a country with a wide range of beauty. Majestic mountains and beautiful sun baked beaches are rivaled only by the wonderful people that you meet . As a family we had traveled to Puerto Vallarta on the west coast of Mexico. It was April of the year that Hale-Bop the comet was making its appearance in the western sky. The winter had been relatively long and cold and a brief respite from the ice and snow was a welcome retreat.

After arriving in the coastal city we adjusted to a slower pace of life. Mornings we lingered on the beach drinking strong black coffee and eating warm fresh baked muffins from the food vendors. Afternoons we swam, read books and played games in the pool or played happy hour bingo at the beach side palapa. After a few days we decided to stretch our horizons and we boarded a city bus heading to a nearby water park.

City buses in most Mexican towns aren't known for comfort and luxury. Sometimes windows are cracked or stuck open so that diesel exhaust fumes can find its way back outside. Most of the time buses are crowded with locals coming and going from work or returning home with groceries from the local open markets. We enjoy riding the city buses and have never felt intimidated or concerned for our own well being. After a wonderful afternoon at the water park we took the city bus back to our condo. We hopped off of the bus along the main highway and walked two or three blocks to our apartment.

"Where is our key?"

"It was in the red bag."

"Do you have the bag?" "No, I thought you had it." "Who has the red bag?" "Dad, I think you left it on the bus!" My heart stopped. My new Nikon camera, some money and some reasonably valuable personal belongings along with towels and swimsuits were in the bag in the back of a city bus in Mexico. A boy from Washington State who had accompanied us offered his advice. "The bus we were on had a broken back window!" O boy, I thought, that narrows it down to about 50 or 60 buses.

With the help of an interpreter we explained the dilemma to a motivated taxi driver and the boy from Washington and I sped off through narrow one way streets chasing down bus after bus throughout the entire city of Puerto Vallarta. We overtook dozens of buses only to discover that they didn't have a broken back window. Through the city streets, down to the bus station back around the outside of the city and then to the airport all without finding our bus. After nearly 2 hours of desperate travel and no success we hung our heads in defeat. I realized that by this time our bag would have been opened and emptied anyway so there was little point in continuing. With a feeble attempt at speaking Spanish I indicated to the driver to return home. I had given up.

As he turned the taxi around and headed home the boy from Washington suddenly spoke up. "There it is, that's the bus!" The taxi driver screeched to a halt in front of the bus forcing it to stop. The driver jumped out and forced open the passenger door of the bus to speak to the bus driver. All of the passengers became quiet as I entered through the front door and looked toward the seat with the broken window. There sitting in the back of the bus was a man in a white suit with a full sized harp in the aisle. He smiled and held up my red bag with everything accounted for.

Angel? Concert harpist on a city bus in Mexico? I will never know. I tried to get one last look at him through the dirty cracked window but he disappeared in a cloud of diesel exhaust.

Ella and Lily enjoying the last days of summer

Life's a Butter Dream

Summertime, sweet summertime, while not my favorite season, it certainly ranks in the top four. Summer is the season for adventure. Plans, written and reviewed through the winter and spring are brought to fruition during that glorious season known as summer. Summer is the season for fun. Baseball games, picnics and back yard campouts fill our free time as work and other priorities get pushed into tomorrow. Summertime is the time to relax and enjoy some of the fruits of your work. There is something very satisfying about relaxing in the shade with cold drinks, friends and no schedule to interrupt your thoughts.

Summer is also a mad dash to the finish. Life here in the upper Midwest seems to leap from season to season with such quickness that it leaves us little time to think. It seems that as soon as we finish putting the snow shovels away, we look around and realize that the maple leaves are starting to turn red. Life becomes a blur as we try to take it all in.

I am not an advocate for laziness but if I had to choose between that and busyness, I would lean toward the first every time. Laziness however implies a definite tendency toward willful avoidance of work and that is not generally considered a good choice. Perhaps a better way would be unscheduled time and a slower pace of living. Unscheduled time allows us to respond to the need or opportunity of the moment. If neighbors or friends suddenly have an overabundance of brats or burgers on their grill, who among us wouldn't like to be able to respond and assist them in their time of need?

We just completed the final weekend of the summer and after our children left it was suddenly quiet. While filled with movement and noise it was anything but busy. It was spontaneous and fun, relaxing and fulfilling. It was an example of what summer and actually life should be. Grilling on the deck turned into hours of relaxed conversation as we talked about anything and everything. Later that evening, in our living room we somehow transitioned into a spontaneous display of talent or lack of talent and then family games. Never was anything planned, but rather it happened as we allowed it to happen in a relaxed and supportive environment. Nearly the entire weekend we laughed and ate and relaxed together and nothing was planned except for one event. The summer canoe trip.

This wasn't a planned route into the back country of Boundary Waters, nothing of the sort. This was simply a slow and lazy trip down one of the local rivers. Most years we head down the Namekagen or the St Croix rivers but this year we went in our own backyard, the Yellow River. As parents, however, we have ulterior motives with the canoe trip. We have found this to be a good judge of character. Two of our daughters were home from college with friends of the opposite sex, one of them rather serious and one not so serious but that wasn't the point. We have discovered that if they could paddle a canoe around sticks, stumps, logs and sandbars in a coordinated and cooperative manner without complaining then very likely they would be able to negotiate other speed bumps in life in the same manner.

It was a near perfect day as we drifted around tight corners in the river and watched eagles drifting high above us in the cloudless sky. Surrounded by friends, grown up children and singing grandchildren, we enjoyed a near perfect ending to the summer. We were gratified to watch them working together without serious conflict. As we neared the final destination our five year old granddaughter Ella, began to sing at the top of her lungs.

"Row, row, row your boat,
Gently down the stream
Merrily, merrily, merrily, merrily
Life's a butter dream."

On that particular sunny Sunday afternoon, I couldn't agree more.

Pillow Talk

Bedtime is that natural time, at the end of the day, when you lay down your daily burdens and begin the transition to sleep. It is a time to relax and unwind from the daily grind. It is a process of emptying the mind, a time to listen and a time to chat about little things.

Children make good use of bedtime. It is story time and when the books run out of pages they ask for more stories or just want to talk about their day. Teens seem to come alive in the evenings. Hours of chatter with friends may seem pointless and irrelevant to parents or other adults but to them it is a time to connect and build relationships.

When those relationships develop into lifelong bonds, pillow talk takes on a whole new meaning. Newlywed pillow talk is muted and truncated by romance and passion but when children arrive these same people resume their nightly discussions with an entirely different emphasis. Exhausted from child care and new duties at work, the talk takes on new meanings. No longer muted by romance, discussions often revolve around car payments, insurance, child care and headaches. One parent or the other drifts off into a dreamless slumber while trying to stay awake. The other tries to let go of the daily grind and drift off to sleep. Both parents seem trapped somewhere between wakefulness and sleep while trying to carry on conversations. Usually about 9 or 10 years after the first child is born, young couples try to regain some semblance of passion in their lives but pillow talk often interrupts. Somewhere in the midst of a passionate embrace one or the other will suddenly blurt out "Did you remember to pay our homeowners insurance premium last week?"

Parenting duties are demanding and it is often the end of the day when toddlers and teenagers are safely locked in their room, when parents have time to talk seriously. "The school principal called today." When your evening pillow talk begins like that you suddenly feel very tired. "Tommy dropped out of first grade to be a computer geek, Suzy wants to marry a rock star with a bone through his nose, and I volunteered you to chaperone for the 8th grade all night dance contest." It is nights like this when pillow talk becomes decidedly one sided. You just turn up the volume on any late night movie and drift into a troubled trance.

Good news starts to be proclaimed during pillow talk, usually about the time the last child is packing for college. By then you have already worked through or forgotten about every trivial bedtime argument over the past 20 years. A good night's sleep is decided, not by crying kids, but by a snoring spouse or a limited number of trips to the bathroom. I am reminded of our own recent bedtime conversation.

"I just love these cool nights with the windows open. I like to hear the crickets."

"Crickets? What crickets? That's your ears ringing again."

"No I had my ears flushed out today, I can hear again. See... when I plug my ears the crickets go away." I paused to demonstrate. "Now I can hear them again."

"Are you sure" she responded. "Well, I can't hear the crickets because my stupid clock is ticking so loud."

"Clock? What clock?"

Communications 101

There is a rhetorical question that bears repeating. "If a man says something and his wife doesn't hear him, is he still wrong?" I don't know the origin of this and I can't take the credit but the answer is obvious. It became all the more apparent when faced with a recent college survey.

I learn things from my children all of the time. When they were small they would repeat in public what was said in private and I learned valuable lessons. Children tell the truth. I also learned not to fight the little battles and everything would naturally work out. If a child hates peas there isn't anything you can do to alter their taste buds. They may relish the dog food and eat dirt but you won't get them to eat real food no matter how hard you try.

As they get older you quickly learn that you don't have all of the answers even if you pretend that you do. Each of our four daughters are learning to function and adapt on a professional level in different areas of expertise. Two of them challenge me with questions and observations in the health care field. One continually out performs me in the writing arena and our youngest seeks to understand how we communicate effectively not only on a social level but on the personal level.

One of her college projects obviously had to do with communication in marriage. Simultaneously she sent us a question that has consequences no matter how you answer. "How happy are you with your marriage?" The answer had to be quantified as a percentage.

You can see the obvious conundrum I was facing. If I answered 100% my wife would know that I was lying. No one is happy 100% of the time. However if I answered somewhat less than 100% I would have to face the equally delicate question about the areas of which I wasn't happy. 50% seemed much too low but I did consider about 80% being a reasonable answer but this still left me defending my position, a situation

I would rather avoid. 90% seemed a better choice but that still left me 10% unhappy.

I was cognizant of the fact that my wife was also answering the very same question at the same time. No matter what I answered I knew it had to nearly match her answer as well. Not only did I have to try and quantify my level of happiness but I also had to figure out how happy she might feel and not just this moment in time but also over the past 35 years. I knew that an inappropriate answer would likely impact her short term happiness quotient and in turn, mine as well.

The timing of the question was fortunate as we were experiencing a lazy relaxing sort of day. I am certain that a bad day would have influenced our decisions. I pondered a bit more and punched in the answer on my phone, irretrievably sending my quantified level of marital happiness. My answer complete, I looked over at my wife to try and determine her level of happiness. She wouldn't tell me.

My phone soon buzzed with a return message. "Ha-ha Dad! Mom is happier than you are! What's wrong with you?" I was stunned. I figured that I had the perfect answer. The only logical answer that wouldn't result in trying to defend my position was 99%. She had answered 99.99%. I think she was lying.

The Road Trip

I carry a travel fantasy around in the back of my mind. I dream about a spontaneous, radical departure from my day to day routine. With nothing more than the clothes we are wearing, we depart for an unknown destination with no agenda, no obligation and no reason to do anything other than the whim of the moment. Eat when you are hungry, sleep when you are tired and leave nothing behind other than footprints and happiness. I even suggested that some Friday night we should simply go to the airport and randomly purchase a ticket to somewhere and live out the adventure. When I shared this idea with my wife, she suggested I keep on dreaming until I come up with something a bit more realistic.

As a couple we do balance each other fairly well. I am more spontaneous and she leans toward preparation and orderliness. It generally works out. She wants me to be a bit more orderly and I have suggested planned spontaneity. Most spontaneous events don't last that long anyway so I can't get into too much trouble. However we have had a couple of road trips that have leaned toward my way of thinking.

The "Great New Zealand Road Trip" was the second of these trips. While Abby was living in NZ we had the opportunity to visit. For several days we did all of the planned things we had conjured up and then there was a lull in our schedule. Packing our bags we headed down the highway on the left side of the road. Somewhat like a pinball we went in one direction until we were forced to go in another. Sheep ranches, rain forests, mountains, wineries, waterfalls, caves, small town eateries, oceans and black sand beaches, we took it all in without a care in the world. For a brief moment in our lives it was spontaneous and wonderful. Our first somewhat spontaneous family trip was a tad different.

When our first born graduated from high school we had the idea to take a family trip before college. A quick visit to the local travel agent indicated cheap fares to Alaska. Fares at the time were $99 per person.

For a mere $600 plus bag fees, taxes, fuel surcharges and exorbitant meal fees we "spontaneously" departed for our 49th state. We quickly learned that the 50th state was the state of despair. It seemed that everyone from the lower 48 had also known of the budget airfares to Alaska and arrived before us. We rented one of the only remaining RV's in Anchorage. Designed for a retired couple with a poodle on a leash, it barely fit our family of six.

Ten miles out of Anchorage we hit a rock and spent the next several hours getting help to change the tire. While patiently waiting for the tire repairs we sat by the highway and enjoyed the sunshine, the last sunshine we would see for many days. As soon as the final lug nut was tightened and the bill satisfied we pulled onto the highway into a cold drizzly rain. It didn't rain all of the time, just most of each day and half of each night.

The great mountain of Denali park was one of our destinations. Arriving at the park we saw nothing of the mountain but set off in search of wildlife. No moose or bears were available that day but we did find a lone caribou that seemed to enjoy posing for photos. The next day was fog and rain as we headed east for eight hours on a pock marked gravel road. The children sang, slept, laughed and cried as the camper narrowly escaped disintegration on the jarring cross country route. Stopping to pick blueberries on the tundra in the rain, one of the older children applied her writing skills to the mud coated back of the RV. "Livin' la vida loca" was scrawled across the mud plastered windows. Living the crazy life described it all.

We caught salmon and halibut in the rain, we watched orcas and sea otters in the rain, we laughed, sang and read books in the rain and in the end we bought post cards to see the sights that the clouds wouldn't allow us to see in person. At the end of the road, 1500 miles later, we unanimously decided it was one of the worst and best family vacations ever.

If you want something to spice up your life, something spontaneous to get you out of the rut of daily living, then hop in the car and leave the map at home. Go where the wind blows and the spirit of adventure leads you. Stop when you are tired, eat when you are hungry and when it rains don't complain. It's all part of the adventure.

(As far as we know, picture is public domain)

Opportunity of a Lifetime

My daughter recently opened some mail and was surprised to discover that the information contained within that envelope was truly an "Opportunity of a Lifetime". It was junk mail and her name was misspelled but how could you overlook something so guaranteed to change your life. It was an opportunity of a lifetime. Really?

I found myself wondering what an opportunity of a lifetime really was and I also wondered if I would recognize it without the accompanying junk mail flier in the mailbox. Madison Avenue makes everything seem like the best thing since sliced bread so it is hard to believe everything that flashes in front of your eyes on the computer and certainly hard to read and believe everything that is delivered in your mail box.

By definition an "Opportunity of a Lifetime" would mean that you only have one chance and if you miss it, that chance is over. Most likely that chance isn't over but the benefit of that chance would surely diminish if you didn't act immediately to secure your place and your chance in history.

As someone who attempts to manage my own retirement plans I have had opportunities of many lifetimes with investing. How often have I studied companies or the stock market and decided now was the proper time to buy and sell. Surely tomorrow would be too late. Vast fortunes awaited me if I only took control of my future now. As quickly as I succumbed to the song of the sirens and bought a particular stock it would plummet toward the abyss, clinging ever so desperately above bankruptcy. Sweating through catastrophic losses I would reassess my situation and consult the latest information available for my benefit. All of the advisory letters virtually shouted to sell now. It was the opportunity of a lifetime to get out while the getting was still possible. Realizing that I had not a moment to spare I grasped my opportunity of a lifetime to hang onto the last few dollars in my IRA. A quick transaction and I was now free of the dreaded stock that was sure to cause ruin to anyone who dared consider its products and services. "SELL, SELL, SELL!" I took my opportunity of a lifetime and sat back with a sense of relief only to watch that same stock price rocket upward bringing fame and fortune to all who invested at the right time. It was truly an opportunity of a lifetime.

Shortly after I was discharged from the Army, I started working at a prosperous eating establishment in the city of Virginia, MN named "Mr. Steak". My position was secured with a tantalizing $4.50 per hour wage but I did get all the steak I could eat. It was the opportunity of a lifetime. I learned how to steam lobster tails, chop lettuce, grill steaks and make chicken salad. The best part was when I was able to hire my young bride as a kitchen assistant. It was the opportunity of a lifetime. We chopped chicken together and wrapped thousands of potatoes in foil for someone else's dinner until one day I grew disenchanted with my position. As a veteran I had some benefits that others didn't have and so I took my experience to the local iron mines in northern MN. My application was reviewed and accepted and within a couple of weeks I received a call. An offer of $12 dollars an hour was too good to be true. It was nearly an opportunity of a lifetime to get hired by the mines. The next week the mines closed due to economic conditions. Apparently management felt that closing now before my first paycheck was an opportunity of a lifetime.

The most impressive opportunity of a lifetime occurred when I was but a young private in the Army. Long before encyclopedias were available on computers, they were sold by sales people desperate to feed their families. I was confronted with an opportunity of a lifetime to gather wisdom, knowledge and a vast resource of information at my fingertips. If I would act now, for only $19.95 per month from now until the end of the apocalypse I could have my very own 36 volume set of encyclopedias. That offer would only last until midnight tomorrow. It was truly an opportunity of a lifetime.

I weighed the risks. If I didn't buy I would be forever doomed to ignorance and cursed to live in abject poverty. I leaped at my once in a lifetime opportunity. Now I would like to extend that same opportunity to you. I have a set of encyclopedias in my garage, hardly ever used but full of wisdom and knowledge. Free. This is an opportunity of a lifetime.

Man Eating Whale

When traveling in foreign countries we try to get a real flavor for each country we visit and sampling the local foods is a great place to start. Some food items may surprise you so don't arrive with preconceived ideas. Americans have a way of labeling certain foods often from their country of origin but if you visit these countries, you may be disappointed. Italian dressing is unheard of in Italy, French dressing is scorned by the French, Canadian bacon doesn't exist north of the border and Danish pastry is a bit different than what is served here. When traveling in Thailand we were offered American fried rice. Naturally we had never heard of such a thing so we investigated. American fried rice is simply fried rice with cut up hot dogs. Apparently Thai's have a good understanding of the American diet.

On a recent voyage to the Scandinavian countries we enjoyed visiting the local restaurants to try their offerings. First of all we found out that Norwegians love the restaurant "TGIFridays" which is an export from the US. We found many such eating establishments on our ventures through the cities. McDonalds also seems to exist in every country around the world. Since these were clearly exports from our own country we avoided them and went to the local locations.

Dining out in Norway is not significantly different than here except you need to learn to say "Uff Da!" Not because it has anything to do with dining out, but rather it helps you to prepare for the cost. Thankfully everything was priced in Kroner so you don't really feel the impact until you get home. I could work out the conversion in my head but this required two credit cards and a calculator. I chose simply to enjoy the food and the setting and pay for it with the play money in my wallet. A sampling of prices would be as follows. Hamburger $150 NOK (Norwegian Kroner); Coke $25NOK; Shrimp dinner $180 NOK; and for you beer drinkers out there imported beer (Budweiser) $65 NOK. Since it was all monopoly money anyway it didn't really phase us until we did the math. Six to one is the conversion so that simple cheeseburger and fries was slightly more than twenty bucks. Throw in a beverage and lunch for two was a typical $60-70 ticket. Uff Da.

One item on the menu that intrigued me was whale. I haven't seen it offered anywhere here in northern Wisconsin so at a seaside outdoor restaurant in Norway, I tried it. I was curious as to what type of whale it was but no one was sure. Obviously with beef there are different qualities of cattle such as Black Angus or Hereford or even old Holstein but apparently whales aren't categorized that way. Likewise cattle offer differing cuts varying in quality and price. You could order a New York strip or a porterhouse or fillet mignon but not so with whales. I ordered the whale steak because when in Norway do as the Norwegians do. Actually I didn't see anyone else in Norway eating the whale so maybe I should have stayed with TGIFridays.

Since I was investigating the local flavors, my beloved wife decided to indulge herself in the locally caught Norwegian lobster. Our tall blonde server assured us that these were fine choices, however she quickly returned to our table, inquiring about the size of the lobster required. Norwegian lobsters differ from their North American counterparts because they are priced by the gram and weighed out with gold nuggets to counterbalance the scale. I checked my supply of monopoly money and she decided a modest sized one would do just fine.

The meal was great in many ways. Unique and tasty we enjoyed it all. The lobster was served chilled with different types of sauces blended with mayonnaise that offered a distinct difference from the usual hot steaming lobster dripping with butter. The whale steak was far different than expected. I anticipated something greasy but it was very lean and deep red and was cooked medium rare to avoid toughness according to our server. I sliced off a corner and was surprise by the tenderness. The flavor however was vastly different than any land animal I had eaten, and I have tried many. I suspect it may have been similar to an old goat who had dined on garbage for years and was left to age in a warm place. I thoughtfully chewed for a minute before swallowing.

"Well...How is it?" she asked from across the table. Rather than answering I simply smiled and offered her a slice. In a nice restaurant it is hard to gag politely but she did it. The cost for our local flavors was rounded out to $1100 NOK. We had a whale of a time.

Sleepless in Oslo

It wasn't until jet aircraft were invented, that we discovered jet lag. Now we can literally travel so fast that our bodies leave our brains behind. Before airline travel we were just tired. Now we have jet lag. It sounds more sophisticated and exotic if we have jet lag. It implies that we have been somewhere. I have a good friend that must suffer from nearly permanent jet lag. Just when his brain catches up with his body, he is off again while his brains plods along, sometimes an ocean or two behind. Such was the problem we recently experienced on a trip to Scandinavia.

Oslo Norway was our destination. We left Minneapolis in the evening with the plans to switch planes in Iceland. This was helpful because while we were delayed in beautiful exotic Iceland, our brains had made it about as far as Cleveland or perhaps Pittsburg. If we hadn't had a delay in Iceland our brains would have only made it as far as Detroit so this was helpful. After three hours of pacing the halls, looking out the windows on the treeless tundra and wondering if I really should try the whale jerky at the snack bar, we were finally on the second leg of the trip set to arrive in Oslo sometime in the early afternoon.

Actually Iceland is an interesting country. According to a family tree outlined by my grandmother, I have a streak of Icelandic somewhere in my past. Actually in Iceland they don't have trees so I guess it was more like a family shrub but we do have roots. On the return trip we also had a delay in Iceland. It was so long that I fell in love with the country and bought a t-shirt that says "I Love Iceland". My wife has already threatened to use it as a cleaning rag.

Oslo Norway is a wonderful city full of Norwegians and a few others who fly in and out or come ashore through the Oslo fjords. The rugged, rocky shores covered with birch trees and pines are strikingly familiar to our own Lake Superior. In fact, when people speak, they all sound like they are from Duluth. We felt at home.

Our hotel was older, apparently they haven't built many new hotels since Norway declared independence from Sweden in 1905. Our hotel was wonderful in many ways except it didn't have any modern way of controlling the temperature in the room. One hotel employee explained that we could play with the thermostat all we wanted but it didn't change the temperature in the room. That was controlled downstairs. If we wanted it cooler, we had to open the windows. If we wanted it warmer we had to close the windows. Simple and effective.

Our bodies were in Oslo but our brains were still only slightly east of New York when it was bed time. We were exhausted and ready to sleep. The room was warm so I went to the 5th floor window and opened them up to breath in the fresh air from the harbor and look down into the street below. Young mothers, side by side, pushed sleeping infants in baby carriages on the cobblestone streets below. Several shoppers causally wandered into and out of the shops. McDonalds, the American dining experience was across the street and next to it was a dark storefront and a sign. Part of it read "Dr". I felt secure knowing there was a clinic nearby and we promptly parked our jet lagged bodies into the soft beds and pulled the plush down comforters up around our shoulders and fell immediately asleep.

Oslo is quiet in the evenings, but not at night. The sleepy streets and storefronts came alive after the sun sets. In Oslo, in summer the sunset is very late. People, laughing and talking crowded into the street. Throbbing music echoed in the canyons between the tall buildings, rushing upward until it found an open window, our window. It shook us awake and I staggered to the window to try and usher the noise back outside. I couldn't. The sounds of the street rose as laughter and talking erupted into yelling and fighting. Storefront doors opened and waves of powerful music gushed out, threatening to wash us away. All of this was happening in front of the Doctor's office below. I watched one man punch another and then slowly the crowds dispersed. By 4 am the music quit and I was able to open up the air conditioner again. Peace at last as I again drifted off into an exhausted sleep.

Do you know what it is like when you are awakened from the deepest sleep, when you are perhaps just a notch or two from death? Within an hour from the end of the last street fight, that is where I found myself. So deep was my sleep that I couldn't orient myself when I heard the next rush of noise. Jumping to the air conditioner, I looked down at the street below as a street sweeper made his way slowly up the narrow cobblestone pavement. It was then I noticed the true sign on the clinic below. "Dr. Jekyll's Pub".

Man Theory

Men and women are different. We look different, we act different, we dressed different, and we think different. Recently I was able to test my theories on the differences between men and women. My wife had the opportunity of traveling to Florida with the local high school band and choir students on their spring trip, allowing me to be home alone for an entire week. I decided to test the theory that "If a man does something and his wife doesn't know it, is he still wrong?"

The first concern that most people have about a man who suddenly finds himself without a wife centers on his nutritional status. Many believe that a man can't cook and therefore he can't eat. I'm no slouch when it comes to cooking and would certainly never starve if I had to rely on my own culinary abilities. This however doesn't dispel the misperception that men are incapable of feeding themselves. Thanks to that belief I had plenty of friends willing to supplement my nutrition by inviting me over for meals. After eating 3 meals out with friends I had to decline any further invitations so that I could further test my theory. Back home alone in the evening I could now eat an entire frozen pizza in front of the television while watching all the sports channels that I could find. With a pizza there were no dishes and the dog ate the crust and crumbs; a perfect meal.

The second thing that I did to test my theory was to go around the house and leave all of the toilet seats up. For an entire week there were no complaints and no one unexpectedly sat down on an unguarded toilet rim in the middle of the night with the lights off.

The third thing that a man can do to test this theory is to organize his clothes in a manner that is very easy to recognize. Monday my clothes went in a pile by the side of the bed, Tuesday's clothes were in the corner and I left Wednesday's clothes in the family room because I changed in front of the TV while I was watching a late-night movie. The problem was when I got to Thursday I decided to revisit the organized piles of clothes already distributed around the house. By then I had to administer the sniff test to see which ones were safe to use. Unfortunately my nose isn't as sharp as it once was so I couldn't really distinguish between Monday and Wednesday. Rather than attempt to put them away in any acceptable fashion it was simpler to put them all into the dirty laundry.

As the day of my wife's return loomed on my horizon I swept the crumbs, washed the dishes and put the toilet seats back into the resting position. I believed deep down in my heart that I had disproven the theory. If a man does something and his wife doesn't know, he isn't always wrong. My only slip was forgetting to put out the garbage for pick up on Wednesday. When she returned home to find the garbage full of last week's trash with added pizza boxes I was busted.

With the next scheduled garbage pick-up I was prepared. In the driving rain I dutifully dragged the trash out to the road the evening before, sprinted back to the house leaving the garage door open. Unfortunately we have nosy neighbors of the large black, four-legged type, black bears.

Leaving for work before me, my wife quickly called my cell phone to inform me that our garbage was all over the yard and road. She also told me I had left the freezer door open in the garage.

I picked up the trash in the yard and as I went into the garage I discovered mud all over the freezer and chunks of half chewed frozen meat all over the floor. I can believe she suspected me of leaving the freezer door open. I also can understand that she suspected I had smeared mud all over the sides and top of the freezer and even inside the freezer. It must have been the bite marks on the frozen package of ribs behind the car that made her suspect me. She brings out the wild streak in me.

So what conclusion have I drawn about my theory? If a man does something he is wrong even if his wife knows about it. But we have managed to live with my shortcomings. Now every morning when I wake up the first thing I do is say "I'm sorry" and give her a big bear hug.

Green before Green was Cool

It is now politically correct to be "green". It has been popularized by many politicians, famous individuals and leading thinkers in our culture. It's now the way to think and live. We recycle our cell phones, drive hybrid cars, refill our water bottles and buy our blue jeans with holes already in them so they look recycled. Congratulations. I remember being green before green was cool.

I remember long ago when grocery items used to come in glass. My Grandmother would get milk delivered to her door in glass bottles that were used washed and returned for reuse. Beverages were sold in glass bottles designed to be reused. I remember searching for discarded pop bottles in vacant lots and alleys so we could return them for a deposit and get some money for candy or a popsicle on a summer day. Back then popsicles were 7 cents and a bottle of pop was 10 cents. (Yes I know it was a while ago). Water was free. We didn't buy it in extremely overpriced plastic bottles. As kids, much of the time we drank it from a hose in the back yard.

Our garden was the primary source of our food for the years. It was so big that when the sun came up on the east end it was still dark on the other end of the garden. The kids weren't allowed to do much of the planting because the rows would be crooked and you wouldn't be sure what was planted. Everyone had to participate with weeding, watering and harvest time. There were so many green beans and peas at picking time. It seemed that we spent hours cutting beans and shucking peas but I am sure it was much less than I remember. A lot of the food was canned including vegetables and venison. We stopped putting dates on the jar lids because it was harder to give away food when the date on the lid was a few years past.

We had two types of clothes; school clothes and old clothes. If you went to church, the school clothes did double duty. The old clothes were just school clothes with patches. When the patches started needing patches then were ripped apart and used for cleaning rags or patches for the next generation of old clothes.

Nobody really thought much about recycling because we were reusing anything that had residual value. Food scraps were composted or fed to the animals; paper scraps were fed to the wood stove to heat the house.

We had a small house, one bathroom and one car. If we wanted to go somewhere, we walked, rode our bicycles or shared a ride. Our central air was a box fan in the middle of the room. We thought a carbon footprint was the dirt we left on the rug from our muddy shoes. We lived cheaply and sensibly and never felt like we were suffering or deprived of anything good. We consumed less, a lot less than the average family today.

Consumption is really the key. Today the average family consumes more goods and services than at any time in the past. We are living far beyond our means, both financially and culturally. Our wants and desires have been redefined as needs. The average size of single family home has risen dramatically. In 1950 the average home was 983 sq. ft., in 1973 it had risen to 1500 sq. ft. and in 2008 it was 2495 sq. ft. What was once a luxury is now a necessity. We need three bathrooms, a telephone in every room, cell phones for every family member, a four car garage, three cars and a boat. We buy water in plastic bottles, eat more processed food than natural food and snack continuously in front of 60 inch plasma screen televisions while watching infomercials on how to lose weight.

I was born at a unique time in the history of our country. The world was rapidly modernizing. "Plastic" was the word according to Dustin Hoffman in the Graduate. It was a tumultuous time, a time of unrest and questioning of authority. Some of us had long hair, subscribed to Mother Earth News and listened to Arlo Guthrie. After a tour of duty in the military, my wife and I purchased a small farm that had belonged to my great grandfather. We raised chickens, pigs, cows and had a large garden. We heated our home completely with firewood cut from our property. I devised a solar water heater that heated water for an outdoor shower we used in the summer. Even the three hole outhouse was called into duty. It was a simpler time and a good time but often it was difficult. There was a passionate sense among many that living a simpler life was the right thing to do even if it wasn't popular in the general population at the time.

Living green is more than throwing your water bottles in a recycling bin. It is more than driving a $45,000 new hybrid car. It is more than just being politically correct. It is viewing ourselves not as consumers and owners of the land but as stewards of the land. It doesn't really belong to us. We are given the privilege of using it for a generation but at our passing it is left to the next generation to do the same. It is being responsible for the small piece of the earth we have control over. It is living an examined life where you take a serious and honest look at your lifestyle and decide to live with less. It is having a long term perspective with all of your decisions; spiritual, financial, social and political. It isn't just "living green" but "living right". Our lives depend on it.

The Christmas Letter

Since the advent of computers we have experienced a change in the way Christmas greetings are exchanged. Traditional Christmas cards with a hand written note are becoming less common and in their place are appearing computer generated letters and photo montage's that rival professional standards. Glitzy photos that are cropped, rotated and retouched to remove blemishes and wrinkles make all appear as if we had cosmetic surgery during the past year. Almost anyone with basic computer skills and internet access can now plan, produce and publish cards and even professional appearing photo books at reasonable expense.

While the appearance of greeting cards has changed considerably the content of the traditional Christmas letter has remained about the same. As long as there are relatives, you will get to review in detail the medley of events beginning shortly after they mailed you the Christmas letter last year. These letters often follow two primary forms. If the writer has children still in school you will frequently get the proud parent perspective. "Our wonderful children are the best at everything they do. Sis has been doing advanced algebra story problems since she was 3 years old. She had to give up ballet lessons because she will be performing her 5th piano concerto at Carnegie Hall next month. We are negotiating with the school board to get her into the advanced kindergarten group next semester. Bronco is our athlete. He is six feet tall now and has size 21 shoes. He scored 10 touchdowns in his peewee football league. It helps that we held him back a few years in school so he would be more developed for sports. He says 4th grade gets easier every year." After reading those letters you wonder why your own children are turning out to be such clumsy imbeciles.

The second form of a Christmas letter often reads like an appointment schedule at Mayo clinic. Meant to bring you glad tidings and good cheer you actually feel like sending them a sympathy card when you finish. The most cheerful part is when you find out that Great Uncle Rupert finally got over a bad case of shingles.

Many of the Christmas letters we receive follow the same format, usually with a similar introduction. "Merry Christmas from the Curmudgeon's. Buster sends his greetings too, but he won't be out on parole until June. We bought a big turkey at the Piggly Wiggly so everyone can come over to our house for Christmas. Cousin Fred says he won't come 'cause he broke his dentures and will have to put everything in the blender. We expect to have a good Christmas anyway."

Following the introduction most letters then revert to a diary or journal of sorts. Sometimes it is a month by month accounting of the past year but more often it becomes a documentary ranging from illness to mishap or injury followed by the surgical reports. "In January, Charlie got the big promotion at work but because he was suffering from gout he got laid off and lost his job. It was good timing because with my hemorrhoid surgery and broken hip, I needed help at home anyway. It is amazing how everything works out. With all the money we saved by not driving to work every day we decided to splurge on Valentine's Day. With the two for one coupon and the senior discount if you eat dinner before 4:30 we had a real nice meal. Charlie got sick afterwards but the food poisoning only lasted a couple of days. "

"We spent March and April in physical therapy after Charlie hurt his back shoveling snow. It was good that he hurt his back because his heart is bad and he shouldn't shovel snow anyway. That man is so lucky. We spent the summer inside because I have skin cancer on my nose and shouldn't go outside anymore and he gets hives from bug bites. We heard it was a nice summer."

The obituaries are next, usually beginning with family members that have passed on, but it often includes friends and distant relatives as well. "If you were at Aunt Melba's funeral in August you might remember cousin Fester. When they were spreading Melba's ashes on the back forty, some if it blew in his eyes. He got a bad infection and nearly went blind.

Anyway he died last week. The doctor's thinks that the infection he got in France during the war came back. All this got us thinking, so we bought cemetery plots for each other for Christmas. I liked the spot on the hill by the big pine tree, but Charlie wants to be down in the valley. He snores so bad we have separate rooms now anyway, so what's the difference. "

No matter how depressing the content, the letters always end on an uplifting note. "Remember to celebrate the true meaning of the Christmas Season and if you are ever in the middle of North Dakota this winter stop by and see us. We would love to see you all again."

Merry Christmas and Happy New Year.

Talking Turkey with Dad

This may seem off the wall but when you chew the fat with your kids are you out to lunch? You may want to get the inside scoop but do they treat you like you are out in left field? When they say "hot" they really mean "cool" but when you say "groovy" it used to mean "far out" but to them it means you are over the hill. If you really want to have a heart to heart talk with them, then you should give it to them straight from the horse's mouth, no beating around the bush.

If you really want to talk turkey with your children, you need to be able to think outside the box otherwise all bets are off. Teen language and adult language is not the same as comparing apples to apples. In fact it is as different as night and day. The key to understanding a teen means you must talk the talk and walk the walk otherwise you will find yourself behind the eight ball.

Rule number one when dealing with adolescents is to remain as cool as a cucumber at all times. They know how to push all the right buttons and if you let them get under your skin you could get hot under the collar and fly off the handle. By remaining calm you can turn the tables and pull a few strings of your own.

Rule number two is to speak softly and carry a big stick. It doesn't mean that you are judge, jury and executioner but it does mean that you need to know how to lay down the law. From past disagreements you may have an axe to grind, but remember the real goal is to bury the hatchet. If you have something to say and it isn't politically correct, you may need to bite your tongue. If you have already said something in anger it is better to bite the bullet and apologize. Eating humble pie may be a bitter pill to swallow but hopefully in the end you will come out smelling like a rose.

Rule number three is to jog their memory. Whether you believe they are a chip off the old block or not, you need to accept some of their behavior as being genetic. After all, a nut doesn't fall far from the tree. If you are pleased as punch with your children regardless if they are as sharp as a tack or just plain Jane , you should never try to keep up with the Joneses. Undue pressure on your kids to perform may upset the apple cart but that doesn't mean you should rest on your laurels. You reap what you sow and if you want them to be a class act always take the moral high ground and don't make a mountain out of a mole hill.

Rule number four is listen to them for out of the mouths of babes can come wisdom. If you haven't developed a habit of listening to your children, don't wait until the eleventh hour. Don't be afraid to let them bend your ear.

Rule number five is live with the end in sight. Even if you are healthy as a horse now and have been living high on the hog, some day you will kick the bucket and bite the dust. Before you are ready to give up the ghost and meet your Maker, remember that unresolved conflict in your family can be a fate worse than death. Offer them an olive branch and you will never get the short end of the stick.

Do I communicate well with my children? More than once I have put my foot in my mouth but reconciliation comes because blood is thicker than water. I am learning to get rid of the chip on my shoulder and just button my lip. Talking to kids easy? Nope, it's hard as nails and sometimes you just feel like an idiom.

This essay is dedicated to my four wonderful children, Leah Beth, Anna Laura, Abigail Luray and Billie Kay, each of whom has tickled my ribs, bent my ear and has given me the most honorable title ever, Dad. In them I am pleased as punch.

125

About the Author

John W Ingalls is a family physician living and working in Webster Wisconsin. He has been in practice in the Burnett County area of northwestern Wisconsin since 1992. He is married to Tammy Kay, his high school sweetheart since 1977 and they have 4 wonderful children and 5 precious grandchildren.

Along with writing, he enjoys many activities including travel, hunting, fishing, camping, eating good food and the company of many friends.

Made in the USA
San Bernardino, CA
13 September 2013